Burned

by

Laura Mechem

"**I** can't believe I let you talk me into this," Annie said as she heaved her luggage into the trunk of the car. "You know I can't stand that woman!"

Lisa emerged from the back door with a suitcase in each hand. She dropped the bags on the asphalt driveway and waited while Annie arranged her luggage in the trunk. "Barbara means well, Annie. I think we just need to get to know her a little better. Besides, it was nice of them to invite us to go along. I've never been to Tennessee. Have you?"

"Nope," Annie said. "Never have."

Lisa picked up the bags she had brought to the car. "What did you pack in these suitcases? Anvils?"

"We'll be gone two weeks, Lisa. Trust me, I packed only the stuff we're going to need. Nothing extra." Annie stepped back to allow Lisa the room she needed to maneuver the bags into place.

"Julie says the mountains are beautiful this time of year. The leaves are changing," Lisa added, hoping to convince Annie to give this much-needed vacation a chance. "She's also arranged for us to have our own log cabin. Just the two of us. C'mon, Annie, it'll be fun!" She put her arms around Annie's waist.

Annie pulled Lisa's arms tight around her. "Okay," Annie said. "I *am* looking forward to some time away from Santa Rosa."

Lisa knew that Annie had been under a lot of stress lately and she hoped this vacation might relieve some of the tension she knew Annie had been feeling over the last couple of months. The two of them had only recently completed the purchase of Williams Funeral Home, and in addition to everyday business worries, Annie's mother Sandra wasn't making things easy.

Annie locked the house and glanced across the street to the funeral home. "The funeral home will be fine while we're away, Annie," Lisa assured her. "Now, let's go. Julie and Barbara will be waiting for us at the airport." Annie slid into the driver's seat and started the engine, and soon they were headed to Albuquerque.

nnie and Lisa walked into the terminal of Albuquerque International Airport and proceeded to the ticket counter. While Annie checked their luggage, Lisa heard a familiar voice calling her name. "Lisa Cannon! I knew that was you! I just knew it!" Annie had heard the voice, too, but she decided she would pretend she hadn't. She quickly struck up a conversation with the ticket agent, hoping Lisa would take care of greeting Barbara Thibodeaux for the both of them.

"Barbara!" Lisa began to greet her, but before she could get another word out of her mouth, Barbara had her in a bear hug and was quickly squeezing the breath out of her.

"How the hell have you bee-in, girl?" Barbara asked in a thick Southern drawl.

"We've been fine, Barbara," Lisa said quietly, hoping Barbara would take the hint and lower her voice. "Annie's checking our luggage. Where's Julie?"

"Aw, she done took an early flight to Tennessee yesterday," Barbara said. "Wanted to make sure everything's ready for us. Plus, I think she wanted to visit with her folks a bit before we get there."

Annie had run out of things to ask the ticket agent, so she turned to greet Barbara. Lisa quickly told her about Julie, so that Barbara wouldn't think it necessary to go through the whole explanation again. "Well how are ya, Annie?" Barbara asked.

"I'm fine, Barbara. And you?" Annie asked.

"Been fine, honey. Jus' fine. Fine as frog's hair!" Barbara replied enthusiastically.

Annie had to keep herself from cringing at Barbara's loud, grating voice. In a few moments, they reached the security checkpoint. Lisa and Annie walked through first, placing their carry-on backpacks on the conveyor belt, and after clearing the checkpoint, Annie walked over and sat down on a metal bench. Lisa asked, "Why are you sitting down?" But before Annie could answer, the security alarm went off and Barbara was pulled from the line.

"That's why," Annie said smiling. She pointed to Barbara who was now being shuffled into a special area for an additional security check.

"But, how did you know?" Lisa asked befuddled.

"Just a guess," Annie chuckled. "I figured the loose nuts and bolts in her head would set off the alarm." She retrieved a magazine from her backpack and began flipping through the pages. A voice came over the intercom requesting a female security agent to report to the checkpoint for a body search.

"You should be ashamed of yourself, Annie Proudfoot!" Lisa scolded. Amazed that Annie had somehow predicted this little delay, Lisa watched as Barbara stood with her legs and arms spread while a security officer ran a metal-detecting wand over her. After about five minutes, Barbara cleared the checkpoint, and the three of them walked to the gate.

Curious, Lisa had to ask, "Barbara, any idea what caused the security alarm to sound?"

"I think it was the money clip on my wallet," Barbara replied. She pulled a thin leather wallet from her front pocket and showed it to Lisa. "I didn't realize that it's just *covered* with leather. Turns out, it's metal underneath. That smart ass security lady acted like that was something anyone would know." Lisa glanced back at Annie who was rolling her eyes and shaking her head.

"You have our tickets ready, Lisa?" Annie asked.

"Sure do," Lisa said pulling the boarding passes from her backpack. "You want the window or the aisle?"

"Window," Annie said.

"Okay, here you go." Lisa handed Annie her boarding pass. "We're on row 12, seats D and F.

Barbara pulled her boarding pass from the rear pocket of her blue jeans. "Let's see, here," she said. She looked at her pass and her face lit up. "Well, whaddya know? Looks like I'm the rose that'll be sittin' 'tween you two thorns. I'm 12-E."

At this, Annie's shoulders fell as though a great weight had been dropped on her. She glared at Lisa. "Oh," Lisa said, trying to explain herself, "I thought there were only two seats on each side."

"Naah," Barbara said. "Honey, I coulda told ya that! There's two on one side, three on the other. Great coincidence though, huh? It'll give us a chance to get to know each other a little better."

"Yeah, great," Annie said. She knew that Lisa would hear the sarcasm in her voice, but she doubted Barbara would.

"'Specially Miss Annie, here," Barbara continued. She put her arm around Annie's shoulders and squeezed her like a rag doll. "She's so quiet. Maybe I can get her to loosen up a little." Annie feigned a smile and silently hoped she had packed a bottle of ibuprofen for the headache she could feel coming on.

Four hours and a handful of ibuprofen later, their plane touched down at the airport in Knoxville, Tennessee. As the airplane taxied to the gate, the flight attendant announced that the use of cell phones was again permitted, so Barbara whipped out her phone and dialed Julie. When Julie didn't answer, Barbara said, "Crazy cell phones don't work in these mountains. Glad we don't have this problem back home in Loos-iana. I guess these mountain people ain't as up-to-date on these new-fangled contraptions."

"I guess not," Annie said glaring at Lisa who sat there smiling.

"Oh well," said Barbara unconcerned, "she'll probably just meet us inside the terminal."

When the passengers began to deplane, Annie announced she would retrieve the luggage from the baggage claim, taking advantage of any opportunity to get away from Barbara for a few moments. She returned a few minutes later pushing a cart filled with suitcases to find Lisa and Barbara still waiting for Julie. "I can't imagine what could be keeping that girl," Barbara said. Annie and Lisa could sense that Barbara was now becoming concerned about what was keeping Julie.

But when Julie still had not shown after more than half an hour, Annie stood up. "Where are you going?" Lisa asked.

"I'm going to get us a rental car," Annie said firmly. "Obviously, Julie has been delayed for some reason, so I think we should rent a car and drive to her place. Do you have the address, Barbara?"

"Sure do," Barbara said beginning an immediate search of her backpack.

"Good," Annie said. "While you're searching for it, I'll get the car." Annie winked at Lisa to let her know her mood was improving. Lisa smiled back at her, knowing that Annie now was moving with purpose, and this always improved her frame of mind.

After a few minutes Annie returned with a genuine smile on her face. She was dangling a set of car keys in her right hand. "Okay, let's go," she said.

Lisa got up and picked up her bags while Barbara continued to punch the number keys of her cell phone. "I don't understand it," she said, "I have a strong signal. She's just not answering."

"Take it easy, Barbara," Annie said. "Now come on, let's go. We'll be there soon." Annie and Lisa walked side by side as Barbara, still obsessing over the cell phone, followed a few steps behind.

"I think she's worried, Annie," Lisa whispered. "I've never seen her like this. She's always so brassy and bold. It's like she's retreating into a shell." She paused and then added snidely, "And I thought *you* were the only crab on this trip."

Annie raised her eyebrow at Lisa, and the two began to laugh. Meanwhile, Barbara, still fighting with her cell phone, was falling farther and farther behind, so they stopped at the terminal door to give her time to catch up. When Barbara reached them, she exclaimed, "I even tried Julie's parents' phone number! Operator says it's been disconnected."

"Well, let's get going.　We can't find anything out just standing around here.　How far is this place from here?" Annie checked her watch.

"At least an hour," Barbara said. "It's way out in the mountains.　I've been there with Julie only once, last Christmas."

They walked to the rental car lot and Lisa loaded the luggage into the rear seat of the club cab.　Barbara stood back and looked at the black full-size truck with a green rental sticker on the bumper, and, for a moment, she was obviously distracted from her concern for Julie. "Now this is my kind of ride!　Girl, you *do* go in style, don't you?"

"I just figured we might need four-wheel drive.　After all, we *are* going to be roaming the Great Smokey Mountains," Annie said. "Here, catch!"　She tossed the truck keys to Lisa, opened the front passenger-side door and got in.

"Hmm," Lisa mumbled as she walked around the bed of the truck toward the driver's door. "I guess this means I'm driving."

Barbara opened the rear door and got in. "And full rear seating, too!"

Amused at Barbara's fascination with the truck, Annie winked at Lisa, and then pulled the seatbelt across her lap and buckled it.

"Okay, navigator, where to?" Lisa asked.　She looked over at Annie and turned the key in the ignition. The engine roared to life.　She looked into the rear view mirror at the woman seated behind her. "And before you ask, Barbara," she added with a laugh, "it has ten cylinders."

The sky was overcast and filled with thick, gray clouds and the air damp and cold as the women departed the airport and headed for Pigeon Forge. They had traveled only a few miles when it began to rain. Lisa turned on the headlights and wipers and reduced her speed. "These wet leaves on the road are slippery," she said.

Annie heard her stomach growl again. "I know we need to look for Julie, but...."

"I agree, Miss Annie," Barbara piped up from the back seat. "We need to get some lunch. I'm sure Julie is fine. I think we're all worryin' for nothin'." Annie and Lisa hoped Barbara was right.

Lisa was trying hard to see through the rain and fog that lay close to the surface of the road. "Can you believe the fog? I guess they don't call these the Great Smokeys for nothing," she muttered. "Let's stop here." She pulled over at a small roadside bar and grill. "These little Mom and Pop places usually have good food."

They got out and went in. A young waitress in a revealing blouse, white shorts and tennis shoes seated them at a corner booth with a good view of the television above the bar. Introducing herself as Ellen, she filled their water glasses, handed out menus, and took their drink orders. Barbara watched her as she walked back to the kitchen. "She's cute, ain't she?" Lisa smiled at Barbara's comment, but Annie chose to ignore it.

Soon the waitress returned to the table with their drinks and after taking their food orders, she retrieved the menus and headed for the kitchen. Annie's attention was now focused on the news headline flashing at the bottom of the screen. "Ellen, will you turn up the volume, please?" Annie asked, pointing to the television above the bar.

"Sure, honey," the waitress said. She walked over and turned the knob on the television.

"Shhh!" Annie ordered, "I want to hear this." Lisa and Barbara ceased their chatting and turned their attention to the television news, where a young man in a white shirt and tie stood with a microphone in front of a smoldering factory.

"Authorities say the Finley Furniture factory located outside Knoxville caught fire late last night. Firefighters worked until late this morning to gain control of the blaze, their efforts hampered by multiple explosions of tanks containing lacquer and polyurethane used in the furniture finishing process. The cause of the fire remains undetermined; however, two employees thought to be in the factory at the time of the fire remain unaccounted for. Firefighters and investigators are combing the ashes looking for human remains. The names of the missing employees have not been released, pending notification of family members. Finley Furniture, owned by Thomas Finley, employs 300 locally. We will have more information for you on this developing story on the evening's six o'clock news. Until then, this is Jason Sowers reporting for Channel 7 News."

Barbara jumped up and said, "Girls, we gotta go! Now! Let's move!"

The force of Barbara's voice nearly caused Annie to choke on a drink of ice tea. "What's the matter with you, Barbara? We've already ordered lunch! What on earth is wrong?"

Annie was again growing irritated with her, and her hunger wasn't helping matters.

"Julie's father and mother worked at that furniture factory," Barbara said, her face as white as a sheet.

Annie and Lisa looked confused. "So? What's that got to do with lunch?" Annie asked.

"You don't understand," Barbara added, "Julie's parents are janitors. The last shift ends at 11:00 p.m. They're the only two people who work at that factory at night."

Lisa stood up and walked quickly behind Barbara to the door just as the waitress emerged from the kitchen with a tray of food. Annie opened her wallet, handed her a twenty dollar bill, and taking the tray from her, said, "Ellen, I'm afraid we'll have to take this food to go."

"But, you can't...," the waitress began, but before she could protest further, Annie was already out the door with the food. "Oh well..." Ellen said shrugging her shoulders. She tucked the twenty dollar bill into her bra as the black truck sped from the parking lot.

It was 8:00 p.m. and already dark when Lisa pulled up in front of the home of Jim and Florence Wilkerson. Lisa cut the engine, sat back and heaved a sigh of relief. "How about a few of those ibuprofen, Annie? Driving in this fog and rain has given me a headache."

Annie turned around to ask Barbara to hand her her backpack, but Barbara was already out of the car, onto the porch and knocking on the front door.

In a few moments, Barbara returned to the truck and motioned for Lisa to roll down her window. It was still raining hard, so Lisa only cracked the window enough to hear her. "Nobody's home. You wanna get the luggage while I figure out how to get us in?"

"Sure," Lisa said.

"Now hold on!" Annie interrupted. "We can't just break in!"

"I don't know why not. It's never stopped you before," Lisa said.

"We're not breakin' in," Barbara argued. "We're lettin' ourselves in."

"There's a difference?" Annie asked.

"Get the luggage, Lisa," Barbara said matter-of-factly. "Annie can sit out here in the truck all night if she wants to, but I'm gonna sleep in a warm bed tonight."

Lisa looked at Annie. "Oooh all right, already," Annie conceded. She opened the passenger-side door, grabbed a couple of suitcases from the truck and ran onto the porch.

Barbara pulled a credit card from her wallet and used it to slip the door latch. "Neat little trick I learned from a woman I knew down on the bayou," she said as she pushed the front door open, felt inside for the switch and turned on the light. "She was a damned sweet woman, too. Name was Moriah. It was a shame, a damned shame!"

Annie decided to bite. "What happened to her, Barbara?"

"Well, we, uh, she started out with small stuff. You know, breaking into river cabins on the Mississippi. But she was so good at it, she soon got bored. So she graduated to bank robbery." Barbara stopped and shook her head. "Turns out, she wasn't near as good at robbin' banks as she was at breakin' into river cabins. Poor girl's been in the Loosiana state pen for the last five years. I still love 'er, though, so I try to visit her whenever I go home."

The girls stepped into the Wilkerson house and began taking off their wet clothing as Barbara continued to wax nostalgic. "O'course, now we both realize things *do* work out for the best. Moriah found her soul mate in prison, and I never woulda met Julie if I's still hooked up with Moriah."

Things obviously didn't work out for the best for Julie, Annie thought as she unlaced her leather hiking shoes and kicked them off onto the mat in front of the door.

Seeing that less-than-polite thoughts were brewing in Annie's mind and afraid that she might actually insert some of them into the conversation, Lisa decided she would redirect the conversation. "So, how *did* you and Julie meet?"

"Well, it was fate, really," Barbara began.

Oh, no, here we go again, Annie thought. She retrieved a bathrobe from her suitcase. "Excuse me, Barbara, where is the bathroom?"

"End of th' hall, sweetheart," Barbara said and, then, not missing a beat, she turned to Lisa to finish answering her question. "I's livin' in a little swamp shack outside Nu-*ah*-lens at the time."

This is going to take a while, Annie thought. *I'll bet Lisa will think twice before she asks her another question. How on earth does quiet little Julie put up with this crass, uncouth woman?* She reached the end of the hall and turned the knob on the bathroom door. Amused, but ashamed to admit she found Barbara's rantings entertaining, Annie left the bathroom door open so she could continue listening.

"Julie was finishin' her degree at Tulane. I's workin' on my lil' brother's shrimp boat out in the Gulf at the time. We met at a gay bar down in the Quarter one night during Mardi Gras."

Fate must have been drunk in New Orleans that night, Annie mused.

"I was feelin' low 'cause Moriah had just gone off to the pen. And Julie was lookin' for love. I could tell that little girl's cherry was ripe for pickin' if you know what I mean." Barbara winked at Lisa and laughed out loud.

Annie emerged from the bathroom in a fluffy white robe. She sat down on the sofa beside Lisa and tucked her legs beneath her as Barbara continued the saga.

"She'd never, uh, you know, **been** with nobody. You know, she was a...," Barbara leaned toward Lisa and Annie and whispered, "a virgin."

Lisa, now almost mortified, nodded her head. She knew that Annie was delighting in her discomfort, and she prayed that Barbara would soon shut up, but there was no such luck.

"So I took her home, gave her a good romp in the sheets, and we've been together ever since."

Barbara stopped to take a breath and Lisa jumped in, "Well, Barbara, I'd love to hear more about you and Julie, but I really need to get some sleep and I know Annie's tired, too. So why don't we turn in for the night. That way, we can get an early start in the morning to look for Julie."

"Sure," Barbara said, "I guess we're all tired. We can pick this up later. I'll sleep in Julie's room down the hall. You two can take the spare room upstairs."

Relieved, Lisa picked up her backpack and nearly sprinted up the stairs. "Goodnight, Barbara," Annie said smiling. "Sleep well. And don't worry, we'll find Julie and her parents tomorrow. I'm sure there's a reasonable explanation for all this." Annie made a mental note to include this intentional lie in her next confession. Truth be told, she was very, very worried about Julie and her folks, but she didn't dare show it to Barbara. There was no sense in alarming her.

While Lisa was in the bathroom brushing her teeth, Annie came into the spare bedroom. She picked up the remote control, turned on the television and found the eleven o'clock news. Hoping to get more information on the fire at the furniture factory, she pulled back the comforter, crawled under the sheets and waited for Lisa. In a few minutes, Lisa, now clad in pajamas, walked into the bedroom just as the same fresh-faced young television reporter they had seen at the restaurant appeared on the screen.

"This is Jason Sowers reporting live from the still-smoldering remains of the Finley Furniture Factory in Knoxville. Investigators are still uncertain as to the cause of the fire that destroyed the landmark structure early this morning. Firefighters from the surrounding areas worked hard to gain control of the fire. Efforts to contain the blaze were hampered by multiple explosions of tanks containing highly flammable stain, lacquer and polyurethane used in the furniture finishing process. At this time, two factory employees, Jim and Florence Wilkerson, are still unaccounted for. The Wilkersons are thought to have been working inside the factory when the fire broke out. Authorities have been unable to locate any family members and are encouraging anyone with information about Mr. and Mrs. Wilkerson to contact the local police department."

Annie and Lisa looked at each other and then at the television screen where Jason Sowers was beginning his interview of Thomas Finley, President and CEO of Finley Furniture. He was a slightly built man in a three-piece suit, bald with sprouts of gray hair over his ears. He looked slightly uncomfortable in front of the camera. Jason threw him an easy question to start: "Mr. Finley, your company has long been one of the largest employers in Knox County. Can you give us some insight into your thoughts about the future of your business?"

"Well, we are obviously saddened by the destruction of the factory, but we are more concerned about Jim and Florence Wilkerson, who have been loyal employees here at Finley since 1974. We are praying they somehow escaped this tragic fire, but at this time we just don't know. As for the future of Finley Furniture, it would not be appropriate for me to speculate about plans for reconstruction. However, I will remind your viewers that Finley has survived two other factory fires in the last fifteen years, and I fully expect we will rebuild."

"Two other fires in fifteen years?" Annie asked. "Do you know what the odds are of having three accidental fires in one location in fifteen years?"

"No, I don't," Lisa admitted. "What are the odds?"

"Well, I don't know exactly, but it has to be highly unlikely!" Annie exclaimed.

"Then again, maybe they weren't *accidental* fires," Lisa mused.

"Exactly," Annie said. She reached over and turned out the light. "Let's get some sleep. I have a feeling tomorrow is going to be a rough day." She found Lisa in the darkness and kissed her lightly on the lips.

"Goodnight, Annie," Lisa said. "I love you."

"You, too," Annie said. She lay there for a few seconds and then blurted, "We'll have our own log cabin. Just the two of us. C'mon Annie, it'll be fun!"

"Funny, Annie, verrry funny," Lisa said. "Now let's get some sleep."

The next morning Annie was up by 7:00 a.m. She showered, dressed and went downstairs to the kitchen to find some coffee. She hoped Mr. and Mrs. Wilkerson were coffee drinkers or at least kept some in the house. Lisa was still sound asleep and Annie decided she would not disturb her. She knew that Lisa was worn out from driving in the fog and rain the day before. Annie was also hoping to enjoy a few quiet minutes by herself before Barbara got up.

She walked softly down the wooden stairs in her sock feet, doing her best to avoid unnecessary noise that might wake Barbara, but she arrived in the kitchen to find that all her efforts had been for naught.

"Morning, sugar!" Barbara exclaimed as Annie rounded the corner into the kitchen.

Annie was careful not to let her facial expression reveal the disappointment she felt that Barbara was already up and about. "Good morning, Barbara," Annie said softly. "I didn't think you'd be up this early."

"Who? Me? I'm an early riser. Always have been!" Barbara said. "I thought you two would be sleepin' late. You know, get in a little morning roll in the hay."

Annie decided to ignore Barbara's remark. "Uh, do you know if there's any coffee?"

"In the cabinet over the sink, honey," Barbara said. "Filters should be in there, too."

Annie retrieved a can of Maxwell House and a coffee filter from the cabinet, located the coffeemaker on the counter, poured water in and set it to brew. Then she sat down at the table across from Barbara. "So where do we begin the search for Julie and her folks?"

"I's hopin' you'd have some idea where to start," Barbara replied. "Lisa says you're as much of a detective as you are a funeral director."

Annie smiled. "I think Lisa might be just a little bit prejudiced." They sat in silence for a few moments before Annie spoke again. "Tell me what Julie told you before she flew here on Wednesday."

"Well," Barbara began, "Flo, Julie's mom, called her the night before. Uh, that was Tuesday night, I guess. I could tell by the way Julie was talkin' that Flo was worked up 'bout somethin'. 'Course that's nothin' unusual. I heard them talkin' somethin' about her parents' retirement and whether they'd have enough money. Julie told her not to worry and they could talk about it when she got here. Anyway, whatever it was, it made Julie decide to come here a day earlier than she'd planned. I didn't think nothin' of it 'cause, like Julie always says, Flo's a high-strung sort. Gets excited over nothin', calls Julie every little whip stitch, and it's usually nothin' big."

Annie got up from the table and poured herself a cup of coffee and then turned to Barbara, "Coffee?"

"Don't mind if I do," Barbara said.

Annie poured a second cup and handed it to her. Then she brought her own cup to the table, set it on the placemat and walked across the room to the kitchen door. She opened it

22

and looked out into the dark garage. She ran her hand over the surface of the garage wall until she located the light switch and flipped it on. The fluorescent lights came on to reveal a two-car garage containing an old sedan and an empty space beside it. Annie could tell that another vehicle had been parked there recently by the oil stain on the concrete floor. Standing in the doorway, she turned back to Barbara who was still seated at the table swigging coffee. "Any idea how many vehicles the Wilkersons have?"

"I think her mom has an old brown four-door. And her dad drives a little blue Toyota pickup. I'll bet that thing is close to thirty years old, but he keeps it runnin' good. They don't drive nothin' fancy, that's for sure. Why?" Barbara took the last gulp of coffee and got up to pour herself a second cup.

"Because the truck's gone," Annie said. "It's not in the garage and it's not in the driveway."

"Maybe Jim drove it to the factory. He usually drove him and Flo to work in the truck."

Annie sat down at the kitchen table again to enjoy her coffee. She lifted the cup to her lips just as Lisa appeared in the doorway, sleepy-eyed and still in her pajamas. Annie glanced at the clock on the kitchen wall: 7:30. "What are you doing up so early? I tried to be quiet so I wouldn't disturb your sleep."

"We need to start looking for Julie." Still rubbing the sleep from her eyes, Lisa walked groggily to the counter, poured a cup of coffee for herself and sat down at the end of the table.

Annie turned her attention back to Barbara, "Do you know if Julie was planning to rent a car at the airport?"

"Not sure. She didn't say. Sometimes she would rent a car and sometimes Jim would pick her up at the airport. But I know she didn't like to ask her folks to drive all the way to Knoxville to get her."

"She would have had to present a credit card to rent a car, right?" Lisa interjected.

"That's right," Annie said. "Unfortunately, we don't have any of her credit card information to find out."

"Now there's where you'd be wrong," Barbara smiled. She reached into her pocket and retrieved her wallet. "Julie and I have a joint account." She pulled out a Mastercard and showed it to Annie.

"Okay, great! Barbara," Annie said. "You call the credit card company and get a listing of any charges Julie might have made after leaving Albuquerque. If she made any purchases with the card, we'll also need the names, addresses and phone numbers of the merchants."

"Yes, ma'am, I'm on it!" Relieved that Annie appeared to have a plan of action, Barbara hurried from the table to complete her assignment.

"I'll get a shower," Lisa said. "And then I, too, shall be at your complete disposal, *madame*." She bowed her head slightly and then lifted Annie's hand from the table and kissed it.

Annie began to blush. "Your first assignment, Ms. Cannon, will be to turn in that black truck for a suit of armor and a

white horse. Now, go on and get moving! Hurry up!
We've got work to do!"

After about thirty minutes, Barbara came into the kitchen with a pad and pen in hand. "Okay, here's the deal," she said reviewing her notes. "Turns out, Julie did rent a car at the airport. I called the rental company and they gave her a blue Chevy Malibu. I spoke with the agent there and he told me the car has one of those tracking devices on it. I explained the situation and they located the car. It's parked in a parking lot at Dollywood."

"At Dollywood?" Lisa asked. "Wow, I've always wanted to go to Dollywood!"

"You've always wanted to go to Dollywood?" Annie rolled her eyes and shook her head as if she couldn't believe what she was hearing. She then turned back to Barbara. "I can't believe the rental car company just gave you the information, no questions asked," Annie said.

"Oh, I lied," Barbara said matter-of-factly. "I told 'em I was Julie, and that I had forgotten where I parked the car. I gave them Julie's Social Security number and her credit card number and they located it for me just like that." Annie sat there stunned that Barbara had been so resourceful. "Well, don't look so surprised, honey! I didn't just fall off the turnip truck! Rental cars were sort of a stepping stone for Moriah and me—between the river cabins and the bank heists. Who do ya think disabled the GPS on those babies before they went to the chop shop?"

"Which states are you wanted in?" Annie asked sarcastically. "No, on second thought, don't tell me!" She put her hand up in front of her. "You might have to kill me later."

Barbara laughed. "You crack me up, Annie!" She went to the refrigerator and came back to the table with a can of beer. She popped the top, took a drink, wiped her mouth on the sleeve of her shirt and then looked again at her notes.

"Barbara, it's only nine in the morning!" Annie exclaimed.

"Yeah, I know." She glanced up at the clock. "What about it?"

"Nothing," Annie said. "Just forget it."

Barbara continued unphased, "Okay, looks like she ate lunch at a Cracker Barrel in Pigeon Forge, and that was the last charge she made."

"And how much did she charge at Cracker Barrel?" Annie persisted.

"Thirty-eight dollars, why?" Barbara seemed perplexed at why Annie was interested in the price of Julie's lunch.

"Well, the amount of her lunch tab might indicate whether she's traveling alone or with someone," Annie explained.

"I don't know, Annie. Julie's skinny as a rail, but boy, that girl can sure put away the food! And don't turn 'er loose in a Cracker Barrel gift shop. It's hard to tell what junk she'd come outa there with."

Annie glared at Barbara and then looked at Lisa. "I think you and Barbara should make a trip to Pigeon Forge and retrace Julie's steps. I'm going to snoop around town to see what I can learn about Finley Furniture."

"Dollywood, here we come!" Lisa yelled. Now even Barbara looked at her as if she were crazy. "What? What are you two lookin' at? I've been a fan of Dolly Parton since I was ten years old!" she protested.

"Finding Julie and her parents is our number one priority," Annie said sternly and then her look softened. "What do you think this is, Lisa, a vacation?"

When Lisa and Barbara had gone, Annie began snooping around the Wilkerson house in earnest. She emptied desk drawers and combed through stacks of mail looking for some clue about what had been going on at the furniture factory. She believed it was no coincidence that the Wilkersons disappeared at the same time the furniture factory burned. And she was convinced that the factory fire was no accident. She hoped that somehow Jim and Flo were not in the factory when the fire broke out, but she knew the odds of finding the two of them alive were not good.

Annie turned on the television in the living room, picked up the remote control from the coffee table and sat down at a roll top desk to see what she could find. She was channel surfing with one hand and flipping through the Wilkersons' Rolodex with the other. When she located the Channel 7 News, she put down the remote control and turned her attention back to the desk. After a few commercials and a handful of local interest stories, Jason Sowers appeared on the screen in a trench coat, microphone in hand. "How about giving me something to go on, Jason?" she said as she rifled through a large file drawer in the desk. She picked up the remote control and increased the volume on the television. Then, selecting a large unmarked file folder that looked interesting, she sat down in an armchair to listen to the latest update on the factory fire.

"Authorities now say that they may never be able to pinpoint the cause of the fire that destroyed Finley Furniture. It took firefighters almost twelve hours to gain control of and extinguish the blaze which broke out around 11:30 Wednesday night. I'm standing here in front of what little remains of the Finley factory. As you can see, there is very little left. Investigators are still combing through the ashes for clues. It is still unclear whether employees Jim and Florence Wilkerson were inside the building at the time of the fire, and authorities are now saying they may never be able to find any remains due to the intensity and duration of the fire. This is Jason Sowers, Channel 7 News."

Annie looked carefully at the screen. Over Jason Sowers' left shoulder she saw what appeared to be a little Toyota truck in the parking lot. She could see that it had been blue only by some paint left on the tailgate; the rest of the vehicle had been scorched white by the fire. "Oh, this doesn't look good for Jim and Flo," she muttered.

"Now this looks interesting," she said plucking a piece of paper from the unmarked file. It was a computer-generated employee benefits statement from Finley dated September 30, 2007, for Flo Wilkerson. She flipped through a few more pages and found an identical one for Jim. Both statements had been ripped up and the pieces taped back together. Annie perused the statements. "This can't be right," she said out loud. She recalled Barbara mentioning that Jim and Flo had worked for Finley since 1974, but the retirement account on both benefits statements showed a zero balance. Same for the 401k accounts. *This must have been what Flo called Julie about Tuesday night*, Annie thought.

Lisa and Barbara pulled into the parking lot of the Cracker Barrel in Pigeon Forge. Lisa got out of the truck. "Well, aren't you coming in?"

"I thought I'd let you do the talkin', honey. I'm not too good at this kinda thing," Barbara said.

"Come on," Lisa said, "we'll go together. You have a picture of Julie in your wallet?"

Barbara pulled out her wallet and handed Lisa the photo. They walked into the restaurant and navigated their way through the gift shop. "Have you ever seen so much useless stuff?" Barbara asked.

"I love it! Wish we had time to shop," Lisa said. Barbara watched as Lisa approached the hostess and showed her the photo.

The hostess shook her head, "No, I don't really recall seeing her. But then again, hundreds of folks come through here each day and to be honest, they all start lookin' the same after a while."

Lisa walked to the gift shop counter and showed the photo to the woman at the register, who hadn't remembered seeing Julie either.

"Well, where do we go now?" Barbara seemed discouraged. She put her foot against the kick plate, opened the door, and then held it for Lisa.

"Now we go to Dollywood to locate Julie's rental car," Lisa said. She reached into her pocket, found the truck keys and tossed them to Barbara. "Here, you drive."

Barbara's face immediately lit up. "Okay, I guess we're off to Dollywood!"

It was two o'clock when they arrived at the park entrance. "Man, look at all these cars!" Barbara said. "How are we ever going to find the one we're looking for?"

"You have a tag number?" Lisa asked.

"Well, sure, but..."

Lisa asked one of the attendants whether cars left in the lot overnight were identified and tagged. Within minutes a young man in a chartreuse t-shirt directed them to Julie's blue Chevy Malibu. Lisa watched the attendant return to his post, and when she turned around again, Barbara was holding the car door open, a piece of wire in her hand. "I think you had more to do with Moriah's heists than you let on."

"I held my own," Barbara bragged.

Lisa slid into the driver's seat and popped the trunk lid. "Barbara, why don't you check the trunk," she suggested, "while I search the interior." Barbara nodded and walked to the back of the car. Lisa took a pen and pad from her shirt pocket and wrote down the mileage. She was checking the glove box when Barbara appeared at the passenger side window with Julie's backpack in hand. She opened the door and slid into the passenger seat. Lisa got out and looked under the front seat while Barbara rummaged through the backpack.

"I wonder why she put the backpack in the trunk. She usually throws it in the back seat."

"Maybe someone was sitting in the back seat," Lisa posited.

"Here, Lisa, look at this," Barbara said handing her a bank envelope.

Lisa read the note on the front of the envelope: Go to Locker #174—Dollywood. She broke the seal on the envelope and emptied its contents into her hand--a small key with a Dollywood keychain attached. "All right!" she exclaimed. "We're going into the park!"

Soon Lisa and Barbara had boarded the tram and were headed for the main gate. "You're really excited about this, ain't ya?" Barbara laughed.

"Sure am," Lisa said. She was unapologetic. "In fact, I can hardly wait!"

When they reached the park entrance, Lisa walked up to a teller, pulled out a credit card and paid for park passes for her and Barbara. They moved through the turnstile, and suddenly it was as if Lisa was ten years old again. She wandered into the first gift shop she came to, while Barbara took the key and went to find out what was in Locker 174.

While searching the Wilkerson house for clues, Annie stumbled upon Flo Wilkerson's car keys and decided to see if the brown sedan parked in the garage might take her into town. She walked into the garage and pulled open the door of the old car. It made a loud squeaking noise. She glanced at the door's rusted hinges. *Jim might have kept his Toyota truck running smoothly, but he sure didn't knock himself out taking care of Flo's old clunker,* she thought to herself. She slid into the driver's seat, her blue jeans wiping away a layer of dust on the tattered bench seat. She could feel the metal springs in the seat underneath her that were beginning to poke through the vinyl, and the dash looked like some automotive earthquake had opened up a wide crack in its surface. Annie pressed the remote garage door opener attached to the visor and from the rear view mirror, she watched the door rise behind her. The old sedan sputtered and coughed, but when it finally fired, she quickly slipped it in reverse and backed out onto the winding country road that had led them to the Wilkerson house.

Annie rolled down the window and breathed in the crisp autumn air. The sun illuminated the bright red and orange leaves that lined both sides of the road. *I wish Grandpa Joe could see this*, she thought. She would remember to call him later. They had been gone only two days and already she missed him and her dog Pixie. Lisa had wanted to bring the bouncy Golden Retriever with them, but Annie wasn't sure the dog would travel well, so when Joe said he would take care of her while she and Lisa were away, Annie had taken him up on his offer.

Annie turned the radio on and found some soothing music. She had spent the morning worrying about what might have happened to Julie, but driving alone in the cool mountain air, her troubles and worries temporarily evaporated in the warm sunshine as she made her way into town. She stopped briefly at a convenience store for a cold bottle of water and a newspaper, the front page of which covered the factory fire.

After a few minutes, she found herself staring at the ashes of what obviously had been an imposing structure. The footprint of the building was roped off with caution tape, but there was little left to look at anyway. She parked the brown sedan next to Jim Wilkerson's scorched Toyota pickup and got out. The driver's window had been rolled down, so she stuck her head inside the cab for a look around. The intense heat had warped the vinyl dash and the urethane that held the windshield in place had melted and dripped on the seats and carpet, leaving the interior looking only slightly better than the scorched exterior. Annie found a screwdriver behind the bench seat and used it to pry open the now misshapen door of the glove box which was empty except for the insurance and registration cards. She checked beneath the seats, under the visors, and found nothing important. She noticed that Jim had left the keys in the ignition for some reason, which she found odd. Then again, she concluded, maybe people in Tennessee were more trusting than they were in the rest of the country. She took the keys from the ignition and looked at them more closely. The key ring obviously contained more than just the truck keys. Annie decided she would look at these later and put them in the pocket of her blue jeans. Disappointed that the truck had yielded no clues, she closed the door and started back to the old brown car when she noticed something in the rear wheel well of the truck. When she moved closer, she could see that it was one of those black magnetic boxes designed to hold a spare key. She turned to go, but something in her gut told her she should give it another look. She bent down on one knee and pulled the box from the wheel well. Sliding the lid of the box open, she found something she thought might be important but it certainly wasn't a key to Jim's truck.

B arbara soon located Locker 174 and retrieved its contents, though she had no idea what to make of what she had found. She was fairly certain it had nothing to do with Julie's disappearance, and she couldn't understand why Julie would have had the locker key in her backpack to begin with. Disappointed that this lead had not panned out and would not help them find Julie, Barbara went looking for Lisa. She searched the entire park over the course of the next two hours and having all but given up, she sat down on a bench near the park entrance to rest. She pulled out her cell phone and was dialing Annie's number when she saw Lisa walking toward her, with a glass of lemonade in one hand, cotton candy in the other, and three large shopping bags full of memorabilia hanging from her arms. "Wanna drink?" she said, offering a sip of lemonade to Barbara.

"Where the *hell* have you been? I have been all over this park for two hours looking for you! Julie and her parents are missing and you are traipsing around like this is some trip to Disney World!" Lisa could tell Barbara was furious.

"I'm as concerned about Julie as you are, Barbara," Lisa replied calmly. "I'm sorry if you thought otherwise. I just wanted to take advantage of what may be my one opportunity to see Dollywood. I apologize if I offended you."

Barbara could tell that Lisa was sincere. "I'm sorry, Lisa. I shouldn't have lost my temper. I guess I'm just stressed out, that's all."

"Hey, no problem," Lisa smiled. "What was in the locker?"

"I have no idea what it is, or why Julie would have put it there. It's just an envelope with a slip of paper inside. The paper has some writing on it, but it makes no sense to me. I don't think it has anything to do with Julie's disappearance. Hell, I don't even know why she would have parked her car here. Looks like we've just been chasin' our tail all day, Lisa." Barbara handed the envelope to Lisa who put down her bags, opened the slip of paper and read it. Then she folded the paper, put it back in the envelope and shoved it into the front pocket of her blue jeans.

"Come on," Lisa said putting her arm around Barbara's shoulder, "Annie's probably waiting dinner for us."

"Okay," Barbara agreed. "Here, let me help you with these bags." Barbara picked up all three bags so that Lisa could finish her lemonade and cotton candy, and together they walked to the car. "You know, I think you're going to have to ship all this stuff home. It's way too much to take with you on the plane."

"Just wait 'til you see what I bought!" Lisa cried with excitement.

A t dusk, Barbara and Lisa pulled into the Wilkerson driveway. Annie was sitting in a rocking chair on the front porch in a turtleneck and sweater sipping some hot chocolate. "I thought I was going to have to go out and look for you two," she said. "I'm glad you're both okay. Learn anything?"

"I learned there's way too much stuff to buy at Dollywood!" Barbara said. She retrieved all the bags from the rear seat of the truck and carried them up the steps.

"What on earth is all that?" Annie said, her eyes widening. Barbara chuckled as she passed Annie and walked into the house with Lisa's Dollywood treasures.

"Just a few things I bought a Dollywood," Lisa said in as nonchalant a tone as she could manage. She walked up the steps and put her arm around Annie.

"A few things?" Annie said.

"So what did *you* find out today?" Lisa asked, attempting to change the subject. She opened the door for Annie and followed her into the living room where Barbara was already seated on the sofa with a cold can of beer, her feet propped on the coffee table. She popped the top of the beer can and took a drink.

"I learned a couple of interesting things today," Annie said. "I found these in the desk." She handed Lisa and Barbara the benefits statements she had found for Jim and Flo Wilkerson. "Barbara, I think this is what Flo called Julie about Tuesday night."

"I don't get it," Barbara said.

39

"Well," Annie continued, "I think Jim and Flo discovered that the retirement and 401k plans they thought they had been paying into were empty."

"How could they be empty?" Barbara was still confused.

"Mismanagement," Lisa said. "I think what Annie is trying to say is that Finley did something else with the money that was supposed to be going toward the Wilkersons' retirement."

"That's right," Annie added. Jim and Flo had worked there for more than thirty years. Can you imagine the panic they must have felt when they learned there was no money in the retirement funds they thought they had been paying into all their lives? After all, they must have been getting very close to retirement."

"I'll bet Tom Finley has something to do with the missing money," Lisa said. "He looks like a crook!"

"I don't know if it was Tom Finley, but he's obviously the prime suspect." Annie pulled the magnetic key box from her pocket. "Then I went to the furniture factory and found Jim's Toyota pickup." She held the key box aloft for Lisa and Barbara to see. "I found this in the wheel well of the truck."

"Isn't that for a spare key?" Barbara looked confused.

"Normally, yes," Annie said. "But this box didn't hold a spare truck key."

"Then what was in it?" Lisa asked.

"This," Annie said. She opened the box, took out a key and read the bright red lettering on the keychain. "It's a key to a storage unit near Pigeon Forge."

"How is this going to help us find Julie?" Barbara asked.

"Just be patient, Barbara," Annie said. "I know you're worried about her. We all are, but I think we have to follow where the trail leads. And I have a hunch we may find just what we're looking for in that storage unit."

"Okay, I guess we don't have a lot to go on, so we'll have to start with what we *do* know," Barbara said. She finished her beer and crushed the can in her right hand. "So what's for dinner, toots?"

"Toots?" Annie raised her eyebrow at Barbara who only chuckled. "We're having spaghetti, salad and garlic bread."

"Yum," Lisa cooed.

Barbara looked at Lisa and shook her head. "Woman, you just had a belly full of cotton candy and lemonade! And Lord knows what else you ate while you were wanderin' 'round that park."

"But I'm still hungry," Lisa said. "And after we eat, I'll show you two all the cool stuff I bought at Dollywood!"

After dinner, Lisa got up from the table and announced that she would do the dishes. Barbara offered to help and so Annie sat down in the living room and picked up the phone to call Joe. "That's odd. No dial tone," she announced.

"I told you," Barbara called to her from the kitchen, "remember, when we were at the airport. I called the house; the operator said the phone line here had been disconnected."

"But why would Jim and Flo have permitted their phone to be disconnected?" Annie asked.

"I dunno," Barbara pondered, "uh, maybe they didn't have enough money to pay the bill."

"No, that's not it. I found their bank statements while I was searching through the desk." Annie pointed to the roll top desk in the corner of the living room. "They're not rich, but their bank account wasn't empty. From what I could see, they seem to be very frugal people. No, they wouldn't have had trouble paying a phone bill."

"So then what was it?" Lisa finished rinsing the plates and put them in the drain board.

"I don't know." Annie stood up and leaned against the doorway between the kitchen and the living room. "I don't know yet, but I'm hoping we can find out." Annie walked to the counter and opened the bottle of wine that she had bought in town. "I had to buy a corkscrew and wine glasses, too" she chuckled. "I couldn't find any here in the house. Barbara?" She held up a glass of red wine and offered it to Barbara."

42

"No thanks, Miss Annie" Barbara said. "I'm just a beer drinker, but I'll sure have a can of beer while you and Lisa have your wine." She opened the refrigerator and grabbed a cold one from the top shelf.

"Great!" Annie handed the glass to Lisa and poured another for herself. "Okay, Lisa, why don't you show Barbara and me your Dollywood treasures?"

The next morning the three women were up early. Lisa made scrambled eggs, fried potatoes and biscuits for breakfast. "You're a mighty good cook, Lisa!" Barbara said as she shoveled in eggs by the forkful.

"Thanks," Lisa said. "Annie's Grandpa Joe is the really good cook, though. He makes the fluffiest, flakiest biscuits you've ever tasted. Mine are just from a can."

"Yours taste good to me," Barbara said between bites.

Annie poured herself a glass of orange juice and sat down at the table to read the paper she had bought the day before. She read the headline aloud, "Finley Destroyed by Fire-- CEO Vows to Rebuild." She read quietly for several minutes and then said, "Listen to this." She began to read aloud, *"This is the third major fire at the Finley factory within the last fifteen years and the fifth in the company's eighty year history. Finley President and CEO Thomas Finley III vows to rebuild the company his grandfather founded in 1927, which specializes in the reproduction of antique hardwood furniture. However, he would give no timeline for reconstruction of the facility. At the time of the fire, Finley employed 228 local residents, all of whom are now without jobs. The fire comes at a difficult time for Finley, which only four months ago downsized its operation and laid off approximately a third of its workforce, citing reduced demand for its high-end handmade furniture attributed to the recent downturn in the U.S. economy. Local officials advise that new federal environmental regulations will make the prospect of rebuilding difficult for Finley, which was already facing an update of its facility to bring it into compliance. Local officials say the cost to build a new facility which complies with federal environmental law will be well in excess of any insurance proceeds the company may expect to receive from its insurer and therefore, will be especially burdensome for the already imperiled company.*" Annie raised her eyebrows as she glanced up at Lisa and Barbara. "Sounds like Thomas Finley had good reason to burn down his factory...again."

"What are you thinking?" Lisa asked.

"Thomas Finley is blowing smoke. I don't think he really intends to rebuild that factory. He may have planned this fire to cash out one last time and recover his investment. I mean, he was facing the prospect of having to spend a ton of money just to bring his factory into environmental compliance. And if he was already raiding his employees' pension and savings plans, chances are he didn't have the cash to do it. This fire solved everything for him. By burning the place down, he collects a huge insurance settlement, uses a portion of it to replenish the money he took from the savings and pension plans, and uses the rest to fund a very comfortable retirement for himself. It gets him out from under a boatload of troubles."

"So what's on the docket for today?" Lisa asked. "What's the next step?"

"Yeah, what's next?" Barbara said looking up only briefly from a second plate of eggs and potatoes.

"Today we explore Jim Wilkerson's storage locker," Annie said firmly. "We can leave right after breakfast."

When the dishes were done, the three women piled into the truck and headed for Sammy's Self-Storage off Interstate 40. It was a small place with only about twenty rental units contained in one long, narrow metal building surrounded by a chain link fence topped with barbed wire.

45

Annie pulled up to the gate, got out and unlocked it with a key she had found inside the magnetic key box in the wheel well of Jim's truck. She got back into the truck and pulled through the gate, and in a few moments, they had located Jim's unit No. 8, written in black marker on the key ring. Annie unlocked the blue garage door and then stepped back to allow Barbara to hoist it up. Barbara grabbed the handle and easily lifted it to reveal a bank of filing cabinets along the rear wall. The women looked at each other and then stepped inside. Lisa turned on the light.

Annie pulled open a drawer on the first filing cabinet she came to and began looking through the papers packed tight inside the drawer. Barbara and Lisa stood there patiently waiting for Annie to speak, but she only chuckled at first. "What's so funny?" Lisa asked.

"Well, it looks like Jim and Flo Wilkerson, two humble janitors, have been carefully documenting the embezzlement of company funds by one Thomas Finley III. And they didn't just start this effort yesterday. Some of these records date back nearly five years." Lisa and Barbara stood there with their mouths open. "It's all here," Annie continued. "Evidence that will send Mr. Finley to jail for a very long time."

"But how did they obtain all this information?" Lisa had a puzzled look on her face.

Annie was still smiling, "Well, as janitors, I'm sure Jim and Flo had access not only to the factory floor, but also to offices and the mail room. One of them probably found something, maybe just glanced at one piece of paper, something that caused them to question or that tipped them off to Mr. Finley's little games. Naturally, after that, they would have been looking more closely at every piece of paper on every desk. Some of these stacks have rubber bands around them with a note on the top that says 'shred'." Annie reached into the drawer and pulled out a thick pack of paper encircled with a rubber band and a yellow Post-It note on the front marked SHRED. "Obviously, Jim and Flo decided not to shred. Judging by the arrogance of Mr. Finley on the TV news the other night, I imagine he wasn't too careful about putting these documents under lock and key. He probably assumed these poor country people wouldn't know what they were looking at anyway. Won't he be surprised?"

"Maybe Jim and Flo confronted Finley," Lisa suggested.

"It's possible. It certainly would have given him motive to burn them up right along with the factory," Annie said. She looked at Barbara who now had a worried look on her face. "I didn't mean to upset you, Barbara. I'm sorry. There's no point in speculating about what might have happened to Jim and Flo, or Julie for that matter. Let's not jump to conclusions yet, but I have to be honest with you, Barbara, the fact that Jim's truck was at the factory, that Jim and Flo were supposed to be working at the time of the fire, and that they're still missing, makes me wonder. I guess what I'm trying to say is that the Wilkersons are likely dead. I know this is hard for you to hear."

"Come on, let's go," Barbara said sharply. She turned and walked back to the truck.

Annie put her hand on her forehead and looked at the ground. "I shouldn't have said that in front of Barbara," she said.

"Annie, don't beat yourself up. You know Barbara had to be thinking it, too. You only verbalized what we've all been thinking. It's not an easy thing to face."

"So now what?" Annie said, unsure of what to do next.

"I think now we need to get some justice for Jim and Flo and Julie," Lisa replied.

Lisa and Annie walked back to the truck and got in. Barbara quickly wiped her eyes and composed herself. They could tell she had been crying. Annie started the truck and the women drove back to the Wilkerson house in silence.

They spent the rest of the day at the house doing their best to relax and come to grips with the fact that, in all probability, the Wilkersons were dead. When evening came, Lisa decided she would barbecue some steaks on the grill out back, and she and Barbara went to the grocery store to get what they needed.

Annie sat staring at the wall in the living room, sipping a glass of merlot. She thought about all the living that had been done in the house, the Christmases Julie must have spent with her parents, the homework she probably did at the kitchen table, the family love and togetherness that the walls and roof had sheltered for so many years. The grief and loss she had experienced in her own family began to flood in on her again, and now she added the loss of their friend and her parents to the list of hurts she routinely recounted in quiet moments alone.

She put her wine glass on the coffee table, got up and walked to Jim and Flo's bedroom. She turned on the ceiling fan light and sat down on the bed. Then she lay with her head on the pillow and stared at the ceiling while she watched the fan blades spin slowly. After a few minutes, Annie rolled over on her side and opened the drawer of the nightstand. Inside were some ink pens, flowered stationery, a Bible and a journal. She concluded she was lying on Flo's side of the bed. Flipping through the pages of the journal, Annie soon gave herself permission to read it, telling herself it was permissible to invade the privacy of a dead woman.

After reading only a few entries, Annie learned that Flo Wilkerson had been conflicted about her daughter's lesbianism. Still, she had resolved to accept it and was encouraging Jim to do so. She wrote of her concern over Barbara's character, wondering whether she was right for Julie, her only child. She believed in God and went to church on Sunday mornings. She loved her husband and enjoyed working with him at home and at the furniture factory. She enjoyed baking, gardening and crocheting.

Annie read the diary all the way through, and when she heard Lisa and Barbara at the door, she closed the journal and returned it to the drawer where she had found it. She would retrieve it later so that Barbara would never read of Flo's uncertainty about her.

Within an hour, Lisa was bringing a plate of grilled steaks into the kitchen through the back door. Barbara was setting the table when Annie appeared in the doorway. "Barbara, did Julie talk much about her parents?"

"Aw, well, she loved 'em, I know that. Julie's an only child so she felt responsible for taking care of her folks. 'Specially her mother. They didn't think mucha me, though. Never said so, but I could tell. They didn't want their baby girl to be a lesbian, but I guess they figured if she had her head set on livin' with a woman, I's certainly not the one they'd a' picked for her."

I guess I won't have to retrieve Flo's diary after all, Annie thought. Obviously, Barbara was already fully aware of Jim and Flo's attitude toward her. Annie felt it odd that each time she thought she had this Louisiana spitfire of a woman figured out, Barbara did or said something that changed or challenged whatever box Annie had tried to put her in. On one hand, Barbara was rough, sometimes even vulgar in her speech, her manners and her attitudes, but if you bothered to look more closely, she had a softness of heart that made the roughness less important. Annie wondered if this was the reason quiet little Julie had lived five years with this woman who was obviously beneath her in education and social background. Both women had had a rural upbringing, but where Julie was the product of hard-working mountain people who believed in the value of education, moral absolutes and a strong work ethic, Barbara grew up rough-and-tumble in the swamps of Louisiana. Here the line between right and wrong was at best blurred and at worst erased altogether, a place where education was never a substitute for street smarts and where people like Bonnie Parker and Clyde Barrow became folk heroes because they were willing to subvert a system that would otherwise have condemned them to lifelong poverty. Annie grudgingly admitted to herself that she was beginning to like this woman who had so repulsed her only a few days earlier.

Lisa placed a steak and baked potato wrapped in aluminum foil on each of three plates while Barbara continued, "Now Jim, he was always wheelin' and dealin', buyin' and sellin', you know, smalltime stuff like auto parts or tools, always tryin' to turn a dollar, obsessed with making more money. He wore the pants in the family, took care of all the money, even the money Flo made at the factory. Gave her an allowance. Can you believe that? He was real quiet, never talked to Flo much. And Flo, she was old-fashioned. She was one of those who believed she was put on earth to take care of her man's needs. So she cooked and cleaned, ironed his clothes, waited on Jim hand and foot. If y'ask me, she's more like a maid than a wife. Thought servin' Jim was the good Lord's will or somethin'. But those two never did talk much. She sure never took her worries to him. No, when Flo was upset 'bout somethin', she'd pick up the phone and call Julie."

When dinner was finished, Annie got up from the table. "Let's all go play some putt-putt," she said. "There's a place along the highway on the way into town."

"I never played golf," Barbara said.

"Oh come on!" Lisa punched Barbara lightly in the arm as she walked to the sink with her dishes. "It'll be fun! Besides, it's no fun anymore just beating Annie!" Lisa winked at Annie, who stood there smiling.

"I'll go...but only if I can drive that truck again!" Barbara said.

"Deal," Annie said tossing her the keys. "Now let's get moving!"

T he miniature golf course closed at 11:00 p.m. and the three women played until the manager was ready to turn out the lights and lock the gate.

"Whew-eee!" Barbara cried when she dropped the ball into the cup on the last hole. "Looks like I'm the new golf champ, and Miss Annie you're the runner-up!" Barbara raised her hand high in the air and Annie high-fived her. "Aw, Lisa, you're just off your game tonight, hon! A little practice and you'll be back on the PGA tour!"

Lisa smiled and said, "I just let you two win, you know. I didn't want to beat you too badly! Didn't want to discourage the new player." Lisa slapped Barbara hard on the back like a football player walking off the field with a buddy and then put her arm around Annie's waist as they walked to the truck.

"Yeah, yeah," Annie mumbled. "You didn't want to beat us too badly."

When they got back to the Wilkerson house, Barbara, tired from the golf game, went straight to bed. Annie walked into Jim and Flo's bedroom, retrieved Flo's diary from the drawer of the nightstand, and took it upstairs where Lisa was buttoning up a short satin nightshirt that Annie had never seen her wear. Annie was wondering whether she would find any panties under the nightshirt when Lisa pulled back the bedspread and asked, "What's that?"

"It's Flo's diary," Annie replied. She laid it on the edge of the bed. "I found it in her nightstand."

Lisa laughed, "You've been all through this house, haven't you?"

"Not yet, but I'm working on it."

"Find anything important in it?" Lisa propped her pillow against the headboard, sat down on the bed and leaned back against it, pulling the sheet over her. *Darn*, Annie thought, her mind turning again to whether Lisa was wearing panties, *she knows what I'm thinking and she's just teasing me.*

"It's not so much what I found. It's what I didn't find that intrigues me," Annie said and then gave Lisa a synopsis of the journal's contents. "What I didn't find is any mention of the embezzlement that Jim has been documenting for the last five years."

"Well, based on what Barbara said at dinner this evening, I doubt Jim shared anything about it with her. He probably didn't want to worry her. Maybe he figured she wouldn't understand it. You heard Barbara, he controlled her salary and gave her an allowance."

"You're probably right. It's just hard for me to believe there could be such a lack of communication between two people, husband and wife, living in the same house, especially concerning something that threatened their financial future."

"Don't be naïve, Annie," Lisa said. "I'd say there are probably more marriages like that than not."

"Think so?" Annie said wrinkling her brow. She thought for a few moments and then conceded, "I guess you're right. Just seems odd to me, that's all. This whole situation is unsettling for me. Things just aren't adding up."

"Yeah, tell me about it." Lisa jumped out of bed and retrieved her blue jeans from the hook on the bathroom door. She reached into the front pocket and pulled out the envelope that Barbara had found in Julie's backpack containing the piece of paper retrieved from Locker 174 at Dollywood. "First," Lisa began, "I don't understand how Julie's car ended up at Dollywood or how a key for a locker inside the park was in her backpack. Her credit card charges didn't show a charge for a park pass. And why would she have gone to Dollywood to begin with? I have no clue what to make of this!" She handed Annie the piece of paper from the locker.

Annie read the typewritten numbers and letters: LLC-GO-2-AL-C-724.112 "You need to go back to the park and find out who rented that locker. Surely a person has to show some ID before getting a locker key."

"You know, I never thought of that," Lisa said. "I guess I was just so caught up in exploring Dollywood."

"Yeah, right!" Annie said. "I know you, Lisa Cannon. You just wanted another excuse to go back there! I think you're secretly hoping to run into Dolly, aren't you?"

"Is it that obvious?" Lisa said. She crawled back in bed and tapped her hand on the pillow next to hers, motioning for Annie to lie down. Annie stood beside the bed and shed her blue jeans and shirt. She began to take off her bra and panties when Lisa objected. "That's far enough. I'll take off the rest." Annie sat down on the edge of the bed. Lisa threw back the sheet, unbuttoned her pajama top, got up on her knees, and pressed her bare breasts against Annie's back, moving herself slowly up and down. Annie could feel Lisa's nipples turning hard against the skin of her back and then she felt her mound pressing against the base of her spine. *No panties after all*, she thought smiling with pleasure and closing her eyes. Lisa caressed Annie's shoulders, ran her hands slowly down her back and unhooked her bra strap. She let her hands move forward to cup Annie's small breasts in her hands, teasing the nipples taut with the tips of her fingers. She ran her fingers slowly through Annie's silky black cropped hair, and then, putting her face close to the back of Annie's neck, she inhaled the scent of this woman she loved so, gently kissing her neck again and again. Annie's breath turned shallow, and she began to moan as she sat nearly paralyzed by Lisa's warm, sweet breath on her skin.

Then, in one sudden motion, Lisa laid Annie face down on the mattress and sat astride her. Annie could smell the scent of her lover's passion wafting from the wetness she now felt against the small of her back, and she wanted only to submit to the woman whose long, slender arms now pinned her own to the mattress as Lisa moved her hips forward and back, pleasuring herself against Annie's bottom to fuel her own passion.

Then turning Annie over on her back, Lisa covered her woman's body with her own like a bird preparing to devour the flesh of its prey. She sucked her breasts greedily and then rolling off her, Lisa let her fingers find and explore the wetness between Annie's legs. "Go inside," she pleaded. Lisa pushed her fingers deep inside, withdrew and pushed in again, and again, harder and more relentless each time. Annie whimpered softly, her breath growing shallow as her passion began to peak. Then Annie's back arched and Lisa's fingers felt the throbbing tightness inside that spurred her to push her hand even harder and faster until Annie finally fell back limp, still moaning with pleasure.

The next morning Lisa and Annie slept late. It was 11:00 a.m. by the time they showered, dressed and went downstairs to enjoy a late breakfast. They found Barbara in the living room glued to the television set. "So you two finally made it outta your love nest," she said, not taking her eyes off the set. "Well, you're missing something important. She picked up the remote control from the coffee table, and increased the volume. "Looks like our Mr. Finley has gotten himself whacked." Shocked, Lisa and Annie quickly sat down on the sofa with Barbara to watch the coverage. "Jason Sowers must be the only damned field reporter Channel 7 News has got." Barbara took the last drink from the can of beer she held in her hand, and then set it down beside a handful of empties lined up like soldiers on the coffee table. Concerned about Barbara's drinking, Annie couldn't help but wonder whether Julie's absence was causing Barbara to slip into a bout of depression. In a few moments, Mr. Sowers appeared on the screen.

"This is Jason Sowers for Channel 7 News. Another tragedy has struck Finley Furniture, less than a week after a major fire which destroyed the Company's factory here in Knoxville. This morning, President and CEO Thomas Finley III was found dead inside his Knoxville home. Authorities are currently without any leads as there was no sign of forced entry at the home. The cause of death is currently being withheld pending completion of the investigation. Local officials are wondering whether his death signals the end of the Finley legacy here in Knox County where the Finley family has made hardwood furniture for more than three generations. The late Mr. Finley's son Stephen Finley has been notified of his father's death. We'll have more for you on this developing story as information becomes available. For Channel 7 News, I'm Jason Sowers reporting."

Barbara pressed the 'power' button on the remote and the screen went dark. "Well, I guess that's that," she said getting up to go to the kitchen for another beer. Lisa and Annie followed. "By the way, I went to the grocery store this mornin' and bought you two lovebirds some Krispy Kreme donuts and a bag of Starbucks."

"Barbara, how'd you know I like Starbucks?" Annie asked.

"Oh, just a wild guess," Barbara chuckled as she popped the top on another can of Bud Light. "Me, I'm just finishin' up my own breakfast." She raised the sweaty can in the air as if she were making a toast. "Cheers!" She returned to the living room and sank into the armchair to nurse the last of a six-pack. Annie decided she would have Lisa talk with Barbara later in the day. Annie and Lisa each grabbed a donut from the Krispy Kreme box and offered one to Barbara, who selected crème-filled. "Beer goes great with donuts!" she announced. "Now what are we doin' today?"

"Well, I'm going back to Dollywood to find out who rented Locker 174," Lisa said.

"Well duhhhh!" Barbara exclaimed. "You gals must think I'm dumb or somethin'. I checked with the lady at the locker rental. Julie rented Locker 174. It was her handwriting on the form. She rented it on Wednesday at 4:00 p.m. It said so right on the form. I tried to tell Lisa on the way home, but she was talkin' about Dollywood this, Dollywood that. Hell, I couldn't get a word in edgewise." Lisa was glad Barbara had gotten the information, but she was disappointed she wouldn't be going back to Dollywood that afternoon.

"What time did Julie arrive in Knoxville on Wednesday?" Annie asked.

"Around noon," Barbara said. "Why?"

"Well, she arrived at noon on Wednesday and was at Dollywood at four on Wednesday, but we have no idea where she was or what she did in between those two times. We don't even know whether she ever made it to her folks' house. Julie did tell Lisa that we'd have our own cabin. I assume she made reservations for us. Do you know where we were originally supposed to stay?"

"No idea," Barbara said. "This is news to me. Julie never said nothin' to me about separate cabins. I thought we's all gonna stay here with Jim and Flo. Then again, I left that stuff to her, seein' as she's from around here and all."

"Have you and Julie ever stayed anywhere else around here?" Annie persisted.

"I told ya. I's only ever here with Julie once last Christmas and we stayed right here with Jim and Flo."

Annie asked Barbara for the credit card charges she had obtained from the credit card company. Barbara went to the bedroom and returned with the list. Annie gave it a cursory look and noticed the company had provided details for the last two months of charges. "Can I keep this for a while?"

"Sure," Barbara said, "knock yourself out, honey! Would you gals mind if I take a little nap this afternoon? I'm kinda tired. I guess I'm really missin' Julie."

"Not at all," Lisa said. "You get some sleep and we'll call you for dinner, okay?"

When Barbara walked down the hall to her bedroom, Annie motioned Lisa to come to the kitchen. "Look at that credit card statement." Annie pointed at the statement she had laid on the table. She took two mugs from the drain board and poured coffee in them.

"Exactly what am I looking for?" Lisa pulled out a chair and sat down at the table.

"It's like Flo's diary. It's not what's there, but what's not there that matters," Annie said.

"Just tell me, Annie."

"Julie told you she was renting two cabins, one for us and one for her and Barbara. But there's no record on that listing of charges that she made any reservation deposit. All vacation rental companies require a deposit with a credit card in order to reserve."

"Annie, I think you're jumping to conclusions. Maybe Julie wrote the rental company a check from her checking account. Or she might have sent them a money order. Maybe she used another credit card. Who knows? I don't understand what you're getting at." Lisa had a questioning look on her face. "Why would Julie lie about something like that?"

"I don't know. Why would she park a rental car at Dollywood and leave some crazy note in a locker that no one can read? Frankly, none of it makes any sense." Annie was quiet for a few moments and then said, "Let's call Grandpa Joe. Maybe he can help us figure this thing out."

L ater that afternoon Annie drove into town to find a phone. First she called the phone company to get the Wilkerson phone line reconnected. "Can you tell me why the line was disconnected in the first place?" she asked the customer service representative.

The answer came quickly. "Our records indicate the phone was disconnected at the customer's request. Looks like we received the request last Wednesday. Doesn't say whether the request was made by Mr. or Mrs. Wilkerson."

Interesting, Annie thought. She thanked the representative, hung up, and then dialed Joe's number. After two rings, Joe picked up. "Joe, it's me!"

"Annie, I'm glad you called. I was starting to worry about you," he said. "Yes, Yes, Pixie's fine. She and I were just watching Jerry Springer when you rang. "

"Honestly, Joe. Isn't there something else you could watch?"

"Nothing quite as entertaining," he said laughing. "Whenever his guests start fighting and punching each other, Pixie stands at the TV and barks. So, how is your vacation going, Little Bear?"

"Actually, it's not much of a vacation," she said dejected. She told him all about the Wilkersons' disappearance, the factory fire and Thomas Finley's murder. "I was hoping you and Pixie might fly to Tennessee. We really need your help, Joe." Joe told her he wasn't certain how he could be of assistance, but after Annie coaxed him a bit, he agreed that he and Pixie would fly out to meet them. "I'll call the airline and get you a flight tomorrow."

Joe and Pixie arrived the next afternoon. Lisa took Flo Wilkerson's old brown sedan to pick them up at the airport. Julie was waiting in front of the terminal when Joe walked out with a duffel bag in one hand and Pixie's leash in the other as the Golden Retriever tagged along beside him. As always, Joe's long silver hair was braided neatly down his back. At seventy, he was still handsome in his long-sleeved white shirt, blue jeans and black leather cowboy boots. Lisa studied the proud Navajo man as he walked toward the car and thought how much Annie looked like him. Of course, Annie had much softer features, but anyone who saw the two of them together would logically conclude the two were related.

"Where'd you get this fancy car?" he said laughing as he opened the rear door for Pixie to jump in.

"It belongs to Flo Wilkerson," Lisa said. "We rented a black full-size truck, but Annie needed it to haul some supplies this afternoon."

He removed a bottle of water from his duffel bag and then tossed the bag into the back seat with Pixie. "I hope you girls aren't going to a whole lot of trouble on account of me," Joe added.

"No trouble at all. Annie just wanted to make sure you're comfortable here during your stay. You know how she is, Joe."

He chuckled. Lisa turned in her seat so that she could fawn over Pixie a bit before beginning the drive back to Pigeon Forge. Lisa picked up a brown bag lying on the seat beside her and pulled out the rawhide chewy she had bought for Pixie on the way to the airport. The dog eagerly took it and settled onto the rear seat to chew on it.

"So what do you think about this situation with the Wilkersons?" Joe had gotten the basic facts from Annie, but he wanted to hear Lisa's perspective, too.

"I think it's likely they're all dead. I think Jim Wilkerson confronted Tom Finley about the embezzlement and maybe threatened to expose him. So Finley set the factory on fire with the Wilkersons trapped inside. Julie arrived that afternoon and probably went to the factory with her parents that night, and she died in the fire, too."

"You really think it's that simple?" Joe screwed the top from his bottle of water and took a drink.

"Honestly, Joe, I don't know how else it could have happened. Jim's truck was at the factory when it caught fire. The documents in the storage unit show Finley had motive to kill Jim and Flo."

"But only if Tom Finley knew that Jim was on to him," Joe added.

"Yes," Lisa agreed, "but regardless of whether he knew Jim Wilkerson was on his heels, Finley certainly already had tremendous motive to burn the place down. His company was in trouble. Sales were slumping and he soon was facing a tremendous outlay of cash to get the factory into compliance with new environmental regs. So let's assume Tom Finley *didn't* know that Jim Wilkerson was documenting his embezzlement. And that he *didn't* burn them up intentionally. He still could have set the fire, or arranged for it to be set. Maybe Jim, Flo and Julie just happened to be inside. Maybe Finley knew they'd be there, maybe he didn't. Maybe he thought they'd get out, but for whatever reason, they didn't. We may never know the details, but the outcome's the same."

"But now Tom Finley is dead, too," Joe reminded her. "Murdered, not even a week after the fire. How does that fit into the picture?"

"Joe, who knows what kind of enemies that man had! We'll probably never know who killed Tom Finley, and I doubt whether most people around here even care. I get the impression that he didn't exactly endear himself to the locals. And if he *did* burn up the Wilkersons, then the old man got what he deserved."

"What do you make of that note Julie left in the locker at Dollywood?"

Lisa appreciated Joe's questions because they helped her determine whether she was thinking logically about a particular thing or whether her own prejudices and assumptions were clouding her judgment. "Now about that, I have no idea, Joe. Same for the disconnected phone line. Believe me, that note still troubles me. I know this sounds crazy, but for some reason, I think it's some kind of a message Julie left for me."

"Why do you believe that?"

Lisa pulled a photocopy of Julie's note from her rear jeans pocket and handed it to Joe. "You see the first three letters?"

Joe read them aloud, "L-L-C. Limited liability company?"

"Lisa Lynn Cannon," she replied.

"Now the next three letters," she urged.

"G-O-2. Go to. Lisa Lynn Cannon Go To." Joe was beginning to understand.

"And the last three."

Joe continued reading the letters aloud, "A-L-C?"

"This is where I get stuck," she said. I have thought and thought about this, and I can't think of anyone I know with the initials A-L-C. So, if it *is* a message to me, I have no idea who I'm supposed to *go to*. It's so exasperating! I haven't said anything to Annie about it, though. I'm afraid she'll think I'm crazy."

"You don't have to worry about me, Lisa. My lips are sealed," Joe chuckled. "But I can't guarantee that Pixie won't tell."

Lisa reached up and pressed the button on the remote control attached to the visor and when the door came up, she pulled Flo's brown car into the Wilkerson garage. Joe and Pixie piled out of the car. Annie had heard the garage door going up and was standing in the doorway between the garage and the kitchen to greet them. Pixie ran panting and pawing at Annie. Annie bent down, threw her arms around the dog's head and ran her hands through the long blonde fur of the animal's head and neck. Then she stood up and threw her arms around Joe, kissing him on the cheek. "Hmm," Joe snorted, "Lisa, I think she is happier to see Pixie than she is me."

"Oh, Joe!" Annie slapped his arm in jest. "You know very well I'm happy to see you!" He laughed.

They all stepped into the kitchen where Annie had been working at the kitchen table, the surface of which was now covered with stacks of paper. Lisa glanced into the living room and saw one wall now lined with filing cabinets. Annie stepped into Lisa's line of sight and felt compelled to explain herself, "Uh, I decided to go through some of Jim's filing cabinets from the storage unit. Barbara helped me load them in the truck this morning and get them set up in here. You know, I just thought, there, uh, there might be something in them that could help us figure this whole thing out."

Lisa looked at Joe, smiled and shook her head. "Where is Barbara?"

"Oh, she's lying down. She's tired from moving all these cabinets," Annie said.

"Nooo, you don't say...," Lisa said sarcastically. "You promised to let her drive the truck some more, didn't you,

Annie Proudfoot?" Joe leaned against the sink counter and stared at the floor in an effort to keep from laughing at Annie's predicament.

"Yes," Annie continued, "You know, that woman can lift as good as any man!" Annie thought if she could just keep talking she might be able to appease Lisa, who was obviously unhappy with a living room full of file cabinets.

Lisa turned away, winking and smiling at Joe, and announced, "Pixie and I are going for a walk so you and Joe can talk. We'll be back in a while. She took the dog's leash from Joe, hooked it to the dog's collar and left through the kitchen door.

"Sit down, Joe." Annie pulled out a chair at the table for him, then sank onto her own. "Lisa's mad at me for dragging these file cabinets over here, isn't she?"

"Naah, I think she's just yankin' your chain a bit. Lisa's fine with it. She just wanted to make you squirm a little, that's all. Now what have you got here?" Joe took a pair of reading glasses from his shirt pocket, put them on, and picked up a stack of papers. "Two people working at this will make it go faster, and I'm sure Lisa will help when she gets back from her walk with Pixie."

Joe and Annie had cleared the table of paper, and Lisa was fixing dinner by the time Barbara awoke from her nap and wandered into the kitchen. Annie introduced them, "Grandpa Joe, this is our friend Barbara Thibodeaux. Barbara, this is my grandfather Joe Proudfoot.

Barbara put out her hand. "Pleased to meet you, Joe!"

"And you also," he said extending his hand. "I understand you hauled all these file cabinets for Annie today." He nodded toward the living room.

"Yeah," she replied, "It was no big deal. I'm just grateful to Annie for helping me find out what happened to Julie and her parents. And uh, o'course, I appreciate you flying all the way here to help out, too."

"It's my pleasure, Barbara," Joe said. He pulled out a chair for Barbara and then sat down across the table from her. "Annie tells me you're from Louisiana and that you and Julie have been together for five years now."

"Yeah, that's right," Barbara said. "Ever been?"

"No," Joe said. "No, I haven't. Always wanted to visit New Orleans, though. Was your family displaced by the hurricanes?"

"No, my folks live in Baton Rouge. I used to live in New Orleans. That's where me and Julie met. You know, Katrina really tore the place up. Jus' hasn't been the same since the storm." Barbara motioned with her hand to get Annie's attention but without taking her attention away from Joe. "Honey, grab me a cold one, will ya?" It was all Lisa could do to keep from laughing as she watched Annie compliantly retrieve a bottle of Bud Light from the fridge, screw the top off and hand it to Barbara. "Thanks, babe."

Joe turned his attention to the Wilkersons' disappearance. "Barbara, what do you think happened to Julie and her parents?"

Barbara took a long drink of beer, and then her tone suddenly turned sharp. "What do I think? I think they're all dead, burned up in that damned furniture factory. And I think that bastard Finley got what he damn well deserved! Now that son of a bitch can burn, too...in hell where he belongs!" Her voice began to crack, and knowing she was close to crumbling, she excused herself from the table. "I'm, uh, I'm sorry. Y'all enjoy your dinner. I think I just need to be alone this evening." She got up, took two more bottles of beer from the fridge, and walked down the hall to her room.

While Annie and Joe cleaned up the kitchen, Lisa prepared a plate of food and took it to Barbara who was still holed up in her room. She knocked softly on the door. "Barbara?" There was no answer, so Lisa turned the doorknob and peeked inside. "Barbara?" she called again. She found the light switch and turned on the light. Barbara lay sprawled on the bed. Lisa walked to the bedside and jostled her arm. "Barbara, are you okay?" But Barbara still didn't respond. Lisa looked around for a place to set the plate of food and noticed an open bottle of pills on the nightstand. Suddenly her inability to awaken Barbara alarmed her. Then she noticed that Barbara's breathing was shallow. Lisa placed her hand on Barbara's neck; her pulse seemed weak. She took the broad-shouldered woman by the arms and began to shake her. "Wake up, Barbara! Barbara, wake up!" she yelled. But still she lay there motionless. Now obvious to Lisa that Barbara was in trouble, she began to scream for help. "Annie! Joe! Get in here! Call 911!"

Annie and Joe ran to the bedroom, and while Joe helped Lisa try to rouse Barbara, Annie ran to the kitchen and called for an ambulance.

It was 6:00 a.m. when Annie, Lisa and Joe returned from the hospital where Barbara was now resting comfortably in a private room, her stomach pumped of the toxins. Exhausted from the ordeal, Joe went to his room to sleep, while Lisa and Annie collapsed on the sofa. "I'm just glad you took that plate of food to her room," Annie said. "If you hadn't found Barbara when you did, she would have been dead by morning."

"You know, Barbara has a crude manner, but she has a soft heart. I guess we just didn't realize how much she's been hurting over all this," Lisa said. "I can't imagine how she must feel. I mean, not knowing whether the woman she loves is dead or alive. No wonder she's been drinking more and more. I guess she's just been trying to dull the pain."

"Well, let's get to bed. I need some sleep," Annie said as she got up from the sofa. Lisa slapped her bottom, and in the most masculine voice she could manage, said, "Honey, uh, grab me a cold one, will ya?" Annie turned on her heel, raised her eyebrow, jumped on the sofa and launched a tickle attack on Lisa. Unable to catch her breath from laughing so hard, Lisa cried out, "Stop! Stop already! Annie, stop! Okay, okay, I'm sorry!" Finally Lisa managed to wrestle herself away from Annie's clutches. She sprinted up the stairs with Annie right on her heels.

The next morning Annie cleared the breakfast dishes while Joe and Lisa carried stacks of paper from the file cabinets to the kitchen table. "Put on a fresh pot of coffee, Annie," Joe said. "It looks like it's going to be a long day."

Annie started for the coffeemaker when the phone rang. She picked up the handset from the phone on the wall. She listened for a few minutes, thanked the caller and hung up. "That was the hospital. Barbara's been referred for some intensive psychotherapy. It's going to be a few days before she can come home."

"By the looks of it," Lisa said, "we'll need a few days to look through all this." She dropped a large stack of paper on the table, sighed and sat down. "Remind me again, Annie, what it is we're looking for."

"I don't know exactly," Annie said, "but I'll know it when I see it." Lisa looked at Joe and rolled her eyes.

Annie spent the morning looking through copies of Finley Furniture's bank statements, combing them for clues about what Tom Finley had done with his employees' retirement and 401k contributions. Meanwhile, Joe and Lisa looked through sales reports and profit and loss statements. Around noon, Joe took off his reading glasses, laid them on the table and began rubbing his eyes. "Find anything?" Annie asked looking up from her stack of documents.

"Annie, Tom Finley may have embezzled, uh, misappropriated funds, but he didn't pocket the money. His business was...."

Annie finished his sentence, "Going under. I know, Joe. Finley Furniture was headed for bankruptcy."

"That's right," Joe said. "You've come to the same conclusion, huh?."

"Me, too," Lisa piped up. "Sales were in a free fall. Down more than thirty percent. His credit had dried up. Some of his suppliers had already cut him off. Frankly, I'm surprised the old man was able to hang on as long as he did."

"So he raided his employees' retirement and 401k funds just to keep going," Annie concluded. She leaned back resting her neck on the top of her chair and closed her eyes. "Probably hoped he could somehow turn things around."

"Hoping against hope, I'm afraid," Joe added. "I wonder if Jim Wilkerson realized all of this."

"You know, I'm starting to rethink Jim's role in this situation," Annie said. "Maybe Jim Wilkerson wasn't as shrewd a man as Barbara thinks he was. We couldn't figure out why Jim would have tracked the finances of Finley Furniture for five years without ever confronting Tom Finley or turning him in. *Maayybee*, Jim Wilkerson was just following Finley's orders. I mean, we don't know who rented that storage unit. Maybe Tom Finley just wanted to get the documents that could incriminate him out of his office, so he gave them to Jim who decided to put them in storage."

After lunch, Annie decided to test this new hypothesis, so she called the number for Sammy's Self-Storage she had found in the phone book. A man with a rough, husky voice answered the phone, "This is Sammy."

"Hi, Sammy, I'm calling about our rental unit number 8 at your place outside Knoxville."

"Why, I knew I'd be a'hearin' from you fellas sooner or later."

Annie didn't know how to respond, so she decided she'd just play along. "You did? Why's that?"

"Well, when I heard about the fire down at the factory, and then that poor Mr. Finley gets killed. Why, I just figured somebody'd be callin' to empty out your units."

"Units? Uh, yes, uh, well that's why I called, Sammy. Exactly how many units do we have now?"

"Well, there's, uh, the twenty at the Pigeon Forge facility, and of course, there's those forty up at our Knoxville location."

"So we have, uh, a total of sixty units?" Annie looked at Joe and Lisa and shrugged her shoulders.

"Yes ma'am. Now when did you wanna pick up your stuff?"

Annie had now shifted completely into character. "Well, Sammy, we'll be visiting all the units this week to verify the accuracy of our records against, uh, the contents, uh, yes, the contents of each unit. Once that's done, we'll be in touch to clear out the units and settle our account. Oh, and by the way, our keys to the units burned up in the factory fire. I'm assuming you can issue us replacements?"

"Yes ma'am, not a problem. You just stop by my little convenience store beside the self-storage building here in

Pigeon Forge sometime after 9:00 a.m. tomorrow, and ask the clerk. I'll leave 'em for ya there. Now can I get your name and number, ma'am?" Sammy asked.

"Yes, uh, my name is Annie Proudfoot and of course, I'll be the contact person from this point forward. My number is, uh," she paused to find the number on the card she had just received from the phone company after having had the phone line reconnected, and she read it to Sammy.

"Well, all rightee then!" Sammy exclaimed. "Y'all take care now!"

"Thank you, Sammy. We'll be in touch soon." Annie hung up the phone looking shell-shocked. "Sixty units? What in the world was Finley Furniture doing with sixty storage units?"

"This is just a *wild* guess. Now, I may be totally off the mark here, but maybe," Lisa paused, *"jjusstt maayybee* **they were storing furniture in them**!" She looked at Joe who was laughing out loud and added, "I guess you realize your granddaughter is going to have us hauling furniture tomorrow."

"Noooo, I'm not going to have you two hauling furniture tomorrow." She got up and headed for the kitchen, then turned around, and said with a smile, "I thought we'd wait until Barbara gets home from the hospital. Did I mention how much that woman can lift?"

Annie awoke early the next day. She decided she would let Lisa and Joe sleep while she checked out the rest of the storage units. She gassed the truck up at the convenience store next to Sammy's Self-Storage, and went inside to pay. Sammy had left the keys with the clerk, just as he had promised. After thanking the clerk, Annie got in the truck and drove next door. She decided she would start with Unit 1.

She unlocked the overhead door, grabbed its handle and threw it up. It was stacked to the ceiling with fine, furniture-quality lumber. Annie stood for a minute inhaling the sweet smell of the wood, and then closed the overhead door again and locked it. She checked each of the other units, and they were the same. In each unit were thousands upon thousands of board feet of cedar, walnut, ash, cherry, and red and white oak. *There is a fortune in lumber here,* she thought. Annie wondered whether the forty storage units in Knoxville contained the same thing.

She got back in her truck and drove to the hospital where she purchased a flower arrangement from the gift shop, and stopped at the administration desk to ask a senior citizen volunteer for Barbara's room number. When the elevator door opened, Annie stepped out into the hallway and located Room 328. The room door was partially open, so she knocked gently, and then pushed the door open just enough to stick her head inside. Barbara was sitting up in bed with a remote control in her hand. "It's just me," Annie said.

"Come on in." Barbara turned off the television. "Sit down."

Annie set the flower arrangement on the windowsill. "I didn't know what kind of flowers you might like, so I chose one with a little bit of everything in it."

"Aww, honey, you didn't have to do that," Barbara said.

"I wanted to," Annie replied. "So, how's it going?"

"Okay, I guess. I don't much like bein' on the fruitcake wing, I can tell ya that."

"Do you know how much longer you have to stay?" Annie was doing her best to keep the conversation going.

"I dunno," Barbara said. "Hope I don't have to be here too much longer. I think the shrinks here just wanna be sure I'm not gonna try somethin' stupid again."

"Barbara, I can't really say I know what you're going through, but I want you to know that Lisa and I are going to be here for you."

"Thanks, Annie, but I've never been one to do much talkin'."

"We don't have to talk. I just want you to know that we'll be here to support you, even if you just need a shoulder to lean on......or cry on."

"Thanks," Barbara said. "Thanks for everything. Don't worry 'bout me. I'll see y'all in a couple o' days. Now, if you don't mind, I'm gonna take a nap. I'm really tired."

Annie walked to the bed and put her arms gently around Barbara. "Take care, Barbara. We love you." Annie couldn't believe the words that had just left her mouth or the way her feelings for Barbara were changing. Only days ago, she couldn't stand being in the same room with Barbara, whose crude, often vulgar manner had repulsed her. But in just one week, she had begun to see beyond this woman's rough exterior into the tender heart that had truly loved Julie Wilkerson and was now grieving her loss. Barbara pulled the bed sheet up around her shoulders and turned over on her side to go to sleep. Annie left the room, quietly closing the door behind her.

Annie arrived home in the early afternoon to find a note on the kitchen table from Lisa saying that she, Joe and Pixie had gone into town for lunch. Eager to take advantage of some time at the house alone, she grabbed a can of soda from the refrigerator and wandered into the living room. She selected a magazine from the coffee table and lay down on the sofa to relax, but after ten minutes she still felt restless. Unable to get her mind off the Wilkersons, Tom Finley, and the factory fire, Annie got up and sat down at the roll top desk, a place she found herself compelled to return to day after day, convinced there was something important in or on that desk that she was overlooking.

She pulled Jim and Flo's checkbook from one of the cubby holes in the desk and began searching through the check register. The handwriting was gently slanted, full of curves, the words carefully written. *This is the hand of a woman*, she thought to herself. She recalled Barbara saying that Jim controlled all the money in the house, giving Flo a weekly allowance, but she felt there was no way the handwriting in the check register belonged to a man. She walked to the kitchen and retrieved Flo's grocery list from under a magnet on the side of the refrigerator to compare it to the writing in the check register. *It's the same hand*, she thought. *So it was Flo, not Jim, who wrote all the checks.* She found a box of cancelled checks, and the signature of Jim Wilkerson was written in the same hand as the grocery list.

This discovery prompted Annie to look again through the Wilkersons' personal files. She could find no other handwriting than that which she had identified from the grocery list as Flo Wilkerson's, but in the back of one file, she found a piece of paper that she believed explained why. It was the paid promissory note for their purchase of the house. At the bottom of the document were both their names, but on the signature line for Jim Wilkerson there was nothing but a large black 'X'. *Now it's beginning to make sense*, she thought. *Jim Wilkerson couldn't read or write.*

Annie was still seated at the desk when she heard the garage door open and in a few minutes the sound of Pixie's nails scurrying across the vinyl kitchen floor. The dog plopped down in front of Annie and panted for her affection. "Annie!" Lisa called from the garage. "How 'bout a hand with these groceries?"

Annie was starting out the kitchen door and met Joe on his way in with a large brown bag in each arm. "She said we needed a few things," he said with a wink.

"Lisa, we just went for groceries a couple of days ago," she said when she reached the trunk of the brown sedan.

"Annie, trust me, we needed some things. After all, we have four people in the house now, not just three. Now here, take these inside." Lisa placed a full brown grocery bag in each of Annie's arms, then picked up the remaining two bags and slammed the trunk lid.

While Lisa was putting groceries away and reorganizing Flo Wilkerson's kitchen for the third time in a week, Annie told her and Joe about her day. "The whole place is filled with lumber meant for Finley Furniture. I have to assume the same is true for the storage units in Knoxville. All told, there must be millions of Finley's dollars just sitting there in Sammy's Self-Storage."

"Too bad Jim's not here to tell us what it's worth!" Lisa offered as she organized a shelf of canned goods. Annie and Joe looked at her like she was crazy. "What? Julie once told me that as a young man, her dad worked in the logging business, and then as a sawyer. Apparently, he bought and sold a lot of lumber in his day. Of course, that's before he took the job at the factory in his later years. He had to quit the logging business because a tree fell on him while he was working in the woods. Julie said it nearly killed him. After that he wasn't physically able to cut timber any longer."

Annie sat there with her mouth open, shocked at how much Lisa knew about Jim Wilkerson. "How did you learn all of this?"

"Julie and I talked the whole day when I first met her at the Albuquerque Library. After that, we'd chat on the phone once or twice a week or whenever I would contact her to get information you needed. I can learn a lot about a person in a short space of time. I'm a journalist, remember?"

"But Jim Wilkerson couldn't read or write!" Annie protested.

"Annie, just because a person can't read or write doesn't mean he can't count!" Lisa said. "Remember what Barbara said about Jim's business sense? Well, Julie said the same thing about her dad. Of course, she never mentioned to me that he was illiterate. She was probably just embarrassed about it, I guess. Now are you two just going to sit there and talk or are you going to help me put all this stuff away?"

On Saturday, Lisa took the truck to the hospital to pick up Barbara, while Joe and Annie drove Flo's old sedan to the Knoxville location of Sammy's Self-Storage to verify the contents of the other forty storage units rented to Finley Furniture. Finding these also filled with lumber, they returned to the house where Lisa was fixing lunch for Barbara. "Hey! Welcome back!" Annie greeted Barbara with a hug.

"Thanks! Glad to be back!" Barbara said. "I'm feeling a lot better."

"Welcome back," Joe said and then turned to Lisa, "Got enough lunch for four?"

"Sure do," Lisa answered. "Sit down."

"What is it we're havin' anyhow?" Barbara asked sniffing the air. "Whatever it is, it sure smells good!"

Lisa stirred the pot on the stove with her back to the table. "Oh, it's an old recipe of Joe's. Road kill stew. We found it out on the highway comin' back from the hospital the other night. It was torn up pretty bad so we're not really sure if it's a raccoon or a possum, but it doesn't really matter."

Annie and Joe sat expressionless and waited for Lisa to finish her practical joke. "Well, that sounds mighty good to me!" Barbara said enthusiastically. "We eat that down Looziana way, too, only we usually use a couple o' swamp rats. Meat's kinda greasy, but you get used to it." Trying hard to erase the look of horror she knew was on her face, Lisa turned around and looked at Barbara, who sat there casually sipping a glass of ice tea. Finally, Barbara spoke again. "Gotcha!" she said flatly, and she, Annie and Joe broke out in laughter that Lisa had been beaten at her own game.

A cool autumn rain started to fall during lunch, and the four of them agreed it was a perfect time for a nap. Joe decided he would take his afternoon snooze on the front porch swing, while Barbara sacked out on the sofa. Annie and Lisa opened the front window of their bedroom on the second floor so they could fall asleep to the sound of the rain beating on the tin roof over the porch. Pixie first thought to join Joe on the porch, but when she realized he hadn't gone outside to play, she decided she would rather take her rest at the foot of Lisa and Annie's bed, so Joe got up and opened the screen door to let her back inside, where she ran up the stairs and pawed at the bedroom door for Annie to let her in.

The house was quiet for the rest of the afternoon, but around five o'clock. Joe was awakened by the sound of a car pulling into the driveway followed by a voice he did not recognize. Joe sat up in the swing and saw a yellow taxi cab, a driver removing some luggage from the trunk, and an older woman with gray hair pulled back into a bun and wearing a plaid skirt. She was counting out bills from her purse to pay for her ride. "Thank you, driver. Here's a little something for your trouble." He thanked her, got in the taxi, backed out of the drive and drove away. "And who might you be?" she asked Joe as she walked up the steps with her suitcase in hand. She reached the top of the porch steps and put down the suitcase.

Joe stood up and extended his hand, "Name's Joe Proudfoot, ma'am."

"I'm Flo Wilkerson. I live here. What are you doing here? What do you want?"

"My granddaughter is Annie Proudfoot," he explained. "She's a friend of your daughter Julie."

Panic immediately flooded her eyes. "Oh my! Has something happened to my Julie?"

"Well, ma'am, to be perfectly honest, we don't know at this point."

Awakened by the talking on the porch, Barbara got up from the sofa and appeared at the screen door, her mouth open wide. "Flo! Flo, it's you! You're alive!"

"Well, of course I'm alive! What would make you think otherwise?" She had a confused look on her face. "Barbara, what in the world is going on here? Where's Jim?"

"I think you'd better come in and sit down. We need to talk. Where have you been all this time?"

Annie and Lisa descended the stairs with Pixie right behind them. They introduced themselves to Flo and everyone sat down in the living room. "What's all these file cabinets doin' in my livin' room?" Flo asked. "This place is a mess!"

"We'll explain it all to you, Mrs. Wilkerson," Annie said, "but first please tell us about the last time you spoke with Julie."

"Well," Flo began, "Julie was supposed to come here to visit us last week. I was supposed to pick her up at the Knoxville Airport Wednesday afternoon, but she called me early that morning and told me something had come up, that she wouldn't be able to make it after all. You see, I had learned on Tuesday that there was a problem with our retirement plan at Finley Furniture, and I was all upset about it. Jim said it was nothin' to worry about, that it must be a mistake and that Mr. Finley would eventually get it straightened out. But I was still worried, and I knew I couldn't talk to Jim about it. I needed someone to talk to, and when Julie couldn't come, I went to see my sister out in Indiana."

Barbara interrupted, "Flo, you haven't been by the factory since you left, have you?"

"Well, no," Flo answered, "I came here from the airport which is north o'here, the factory is to the south. I would have had no reason to go by there. Why? What's the matter?"

"The factory burned down late Wednesday night," Barbara said. "There's nothing left of it."

"Well, why didn't Jim call me? Oh my God, Jim was at the factory, wasn't he? Is he hurt?"

Barbara leaned forward on the sofa. "Flo, we think he's dead." There was silence in the room for a few moments, before Barbara spoke again. "Jim's truck was parked in its usual spot outside the factory. The fire scorched it, melted the dash. We're assuming Jim was inside at the time of the fire. It started during his shift."

"But what caused the fire? And wouldn't they have found his bones, his teeth or something?" Flo asked.

"They say the fire burned so hot and so long that there was prob'ly little or none left to find. Took the firefighters six hours to gain control of it. There were some big explosions, too." Barbara stared at the floor so she didn't have to see the tears she thought would soon be running down Flo's cheeks, but when she looked up, Flo was sitting there like a stone, her face devoid of emotion.

"What about Julie, where is she?" Flo asked.

"We don't know. She was supposed to pick us up at the airport on Thursday, but when she didn't show up, we thought we'd find her here with you and Jim," Annie said. "Then, on the way here, we learned of the factory fire, and when we arrived, you and Jim weren't here, and we thought the three of you had died in the fire." Annie had no intention of telling Flo about Julie's rental car left at Dollywood, her lunch at the Pigeon Forge Cracker Barrel, or the cryptic message left in Locker 174.

Flo sat staring straight ahead, as if she hadn't heard any of what Annie had just said to her. "We'll get out of your way here, Flo. Maybe we can just rent a cabin nearby so you can have some time alone in your own home to come to grips with all of this."

"No, that won't be necessary," she replied. "I can't stay here. Not without Jim." She looked at Barbara, "Will you drive me back to the airport?"

"But Flo, you just got here!" Barbara protested. "Aren't you going to stay to help us figure out what happened to Julie? Maybe have a funeral service for Jim?"

"Right now I need to be with my sister. Jim's gone, and nothing I do now is going to bring him back. As for Julie, I need time to think about what to do. You all stay here as long as you like. Barbara, get my car out of the garage and take me back to the airport."

Barbara dutifully started toward the garage, when Annie said, "Wait! Here Barbara, take the truck." She tossed Barbara the keys, and then turned to Flo, "You'll be more comfortable in the truck, Flo. And if there is anything we can do for you while you're at your sister's house, you know how to reach us."

"Thank you, Annie," she said sincerely. "Barbara, I'm going to pack a few more things and then I'll be ready to go." Flo excused herself and went to her bedroom.

When she had gone, Annie walked across the room to where Barbara was seated and whispered, "You've got to trust me on this, Barbara. On your drive up there, don't tell Flo anything about Julie being in the area on Wednesday or anything about Dollywood. And don't give her any information about Tom Finley. Don't mention the fact that we know the phone here was ever disconnected. I guess what I'm saying is, don't tell her anything. The less information she has, the better. I'll explain all of this later. Lisa and I will be just a few minutes behind you. After you drop her off at the terminal, we'll meet you at the little Shell Station near the airport exit. We're going to follow her!

"How you gonna follow her, honey? She's gettin' on a plane, for Pete's sake!" Barbara said softly.

"I have a hunch she won't be getting on a plane," Annie said.

Flo emerged from her bedroom with a second suitcase in hand. She handed it to Barbara who was already standing there holding the suitcase Flo had arrived with. Her hands full, Barbara pressed her back against the screen door to open it and held it for Flo who walked silently to the truck.

Lisa stood next to Annie at the door and whispered, "She treats Barbara like some sort of footman!"

"Come on, let's go!" Annie said. "Joe, you stay here with Pixie. I don't know when we'll be back, but we'll keep in touch by phone." Annie kissed him on the cheek and hurried after Lisa to the garage. They got into Flo's old car and when they heard the truck pull away, Annie pushed the remote control on the visor and the garage door opened. They waved goodbye to Joe and Pixie who stood in the doorway between the kitchen and the garage. Lisa backed the car out of the driveway and the two were on their way to Knoxville.

Annie now was glad she had rented the big black truck, which was conspicuous and easy to follow from a distance. When they reached the highway and were following Barbara and Flo comfortably, Lisa looked over at Annie, who sat in the passenger seat deep in thought. Seeing the wheels turning rapidly in Annie's mind, Lisa spoke carefully, "Can I ask you something?"

"Sure! What is it?"

"What the hell are we doing here?" Lisa asked, her hands momentarily flying from the steering wheel.

"We're following Barbara and Flo!" Annie spoke nonchalantly as if her plan should have been obvious.

Lisa was growing exasperated. "I know *that,* Annie. What I don't understand is *why*!"

"Flo was home only a few minutes, is told her husband is dead and her daughter is missing, and she abruptly decides to leave and fly back to Indiana. She had no questions for us about how the fire started, or whether anyone else was hurt or killed in the fire. She didn't even tell us how we could get in touch with her in Indiana!"

"Well what do you think she is doing?"

"I don't know yet, but I have a hunch she isn't flying to back to Indiana. I doubt she ever went there to begin with. But we'll know soon enough, won't we?"

"I suppose so," Lisa said.

In the black truck rolling along the highway up ahead of the brown sedan, things were much quieter. Flo had hoped that Barbara might disclose some of what she, Annie, Lisa and Joe knew, but Barbara, careful to follow Annie's instructions, gave her no such satisfaction. About halfway to the airport, Flo realized that Barbara wasn't going to volunteer any information, so she decided she would fish for some. "I don't understand what could have become of Julie, Barbara. When did you speak with her last?"

Barbara shifted in her seat and thought before she spoke, "Uh, the last time we talked was when I dropped her at the airport in Albuquerque. I don't understand why she would have called you to say she wasn't coming. Julie knew that Annie, Lisa and I were flying here the following day. Said she was comin' here to get things ready for us."

"Hmm," Flo said, "I don't understand it either."

"If you hear from her while you're in Indiana, please call me. I guess I'll be staying at your place for the time being. Maybe you could give me your sister's number in Indiana, and I can update you with any new information we get."

Barbara leaned back against the headrest and waited for Flo's response.

"I appreciate that, Barbara, I really do," she began, "but to tell the truth, I don't even remember her number and unfortunately, I didn't bring it with me."

"Well then, what's her name and I'll call directory assistance," Barbara offered.

"Uh, I'm pretty sure her number's unlisted," Flo said. "I'll just call you every once in a while. Barbara I'm tired, so I'm going to take a little nap now." Flo closed her eyes and hoped that Barbara would not press the issue further.

Barbara's cell phone rang and she removed it from the case on her belt. "Hello there," she said. She looked over at Flo who was still feigning sleep.

It was Annie calling from her cell phone. "Barbara, it's me, Annie. We're about a mile behind you. Don't let on that it's me. Just answer yes or no."

'Mom! How are you? Yeah, I understand," Barbara said.

"Has Flo said anything to make you think she doesn't intend to fly to Indiana?" Annie asked.

"Oh yeah!" Barbara said, "I think you're prob'ly right."

"Okay, just be ready to get in with us at the Shell Station. We don't want to lose her."

"Sure, Mom, I promise I won't forget to call." Barbara could hear Annie chuckling on the other end of the line. "Okay, love you, too. Bye now." Barbara closed the flip phone and returned it to the case on her belt. Then she turned on the radio and looked for a station.

When they reached the airport, Barbara pulled up to the front of the terminal, got out and retrieved Flo's bags. "Thank you, Barbara. I'll be in touch," she said in a stern, yet insincere tone Barbara had never heard her use. Barbara went to hug her, but Flo had already picked up the suitcases and started for the terminal. Barbara looked up to see Annie and Lisa parked a few hundred yards behind her. She got back into the truck and drove to the Shell Station to wait for them.

Annie and Lisa sat there watching the front of the terminal for about ten minutes with no sign of Flo. Annie wondered whether she had misread the situation altogether when Flo exited the terminal and hailed a cab at the curb. "Bingo," said Annie, "there she is! Now follow and don't lose her."

"I don't know how you do it, Annie." Lisa said as she put the old car in gear and zeroed in on the cab now carrying Flo Wilkerson. "Now all we have to do is hope this old brown bucket of bolts can give chase."

Barbara was standing on the corner at the Shell Station and jumped into the back seat when Lisa turned the corner and slowed to pick her up. Barbara slammed the rear door and asked, "So where do ya think she's headed?"

They turned onto Interstate 40 and followed the taxicab as it wound through Knoxville. When Flo's cab signaled right, Lisa followed it onto the exit ramp, keeping a few cars between them. The taxicab merged into traffic at the bottom of the ramp and moved into the far left lane, turning left at the stoplight. The light turned yellow as Lisa was about to make her left turn. She considered running the

91

light to keep from losing track of Flo, but when the oncoming traffic started to move, the brown sedan was forced to yield. Stopped at the light, they watched as Flo's taxi went only a short distance before pulling into the parking lot of a seedy little motel advertising weekly rates on the neon sign out front. Flo got out and went into the room where she obviously had been staying.

"I wonder how long she's been staying here," Barbara said.

Lisa glanced at Barbara in her rear view mirror and said, "I wonder *why* she's been staying here." Lisa then turned to Annie, "What do you think?" Annie shook her head but said nothing, keenly aware that at this point, she had no facts, just a handful of speculations that she didn't dare disclose because they would only serve to hurt Barbara. The red light turned to a green arrow and Lisa turned left, driving past the motel without stopping.

The women retraced their steps, picked up the black rental truck at the Shell Station and drove back to Pigeon Forge. They pulled into the Wilkerson driveway to find Joe playing Frisbee with Pixie. "She's pretty good, isn't she?" he said after the dog caught the disk in her mouth and brought it back to him.

"Anything happen while we were gone?" Annie asked.

"Just a phone call," Joe chuckled as he watched Pixie chasing the Frisbee the length of the lawn.

"Oh, who would have called us here?"

"Sam Dalton." He could tell Annie didn't recognize the name, so he reminded her, "You know, the guy who runs the storage place."

"Oh, you mean Sammy!" Annie said.

"Yes, Sammy," he said. "He wanted to know when you were planning to clear out the storage units. He said there's no rush, but he wanted to get a head start on the paperwork."

This time Pixie brought the Frisbee to Annie who ran her left hand through her own shiny black hair as she let the disk sail again through the cool autumn air. "Hmmm, that's odd," she said, "I just talked to him two days ago. I would think he wouldn't be so eager to get those units emptied." Joe shrugged. "Oh well, I'll give him a call."

Annie went inside while Lisa, Barbara and Joe joined in the fun with Pixie. She retrieved her wallet from her rear jeans pocket, removed Sammy's business card and dialed the number.

A young woman answered, "Sam Dalton Insurance Agency. This is Tabitha speaking. How may I help you?"

"Uh, I think I dialed the wrong number," Annie answered, "I was trying to reach Sammy's, uh, Sam Dalton's Self-Storage."

"No, no, this is the right number," Tabitha assured her. "Sammy uses the same number for his insurance agency and the self-storage business. I answer during business hours, and Sammy forwards the calls to his cell phone when the insurance office isn't open. What can I do for you?"

"This is Annie Proudfoot with Finley Furniture returning his call."

"Oh, Ms. Proudfoot," Tabitha fawned, "I know Sammy is eager to speak with you. Will you please hold for a moment?"

Before Annie could answer, Tabitha had placed the phone on hold and Sammy's insurance jingle was playing in her ear. She hadn't been on hold for more than a few seconds when Sam Dalton came to the phone. "Ms. Proudfoot," he began.

"Please, call me Annie."

"Okay then, Miss Annie, I just wanted to find out when you might be, uh, thinking of clearing out the units for Finley Furniture. No rush, you understand. You take just as long as you need. I just wanted to make sure I had the paperwork ready in case you were thinking of doing it anytime soon."

"Well, that's something I was wondering about. I've been unable to locate copies of the rental agreements. I guess they may have been destroyed in the fire. Can I get replacement copies from you?"

"Well, uh, you see," Sammy stuttered, "Tom Finley was a personal friend of mine."

"He was?" Annie's voice did not disguise her surprise.

"Yeah, Tom and me go way back. Went to high school together. Anyhow, our being friends and all, we didn't really have any formal written rental agreements. We just did it on a handshake." Sammy stopped and waited for Annie to say something, but when she didn't reply immediately, he was uncomfortable with the awkward silence and just kept going, "Well, you know, Tom Finley was a good insurance customer o' mine. He, uh, had his factory insured through my agency, so I gave him a special deal on the storage units. He needed a temporary place to store some excess lumber. Didn't have room for all of it in the factory, I guess. So I offered my storage facilities to him for a few months. No big deal, just helpin' out a friend."

Annie was glad she hadn't rushed to answer Sammy, for her silence had inadvertently compelled him to volunteer some new and very curious information. For some reason, Sam Dalton seemed too eager to know when the fortune in lumber stored at his facilities was going to be moved. So Annie decided to lead him along. "Well, uh, Sammy, I'm not really sure *when* we'll be prepared to clear the units, I'm going to start inventorying the Pigeon Forge units tomorrow morning, and then I probably won't get to the Knoxville units until sometime next week. I picked up the keys you left for me at the convenience store, but to be

95

honest, I haven't had a chance to look inside any of the units to see how much lumber is left. Do you have any idea how much Mr. Finley might have had stored in your facilities?"

Annie could hear relief in Sammy's voice. "Oh, you know, I don't think there's very much left at all. To the best of my knowledge, Tom already had most of it moved to the factory about a week prior to the fire. I don't think there'll be very much at all for you to have to worry with. Yeah, it's a real shame all that lumber bein' lost."

"Well, that's great," Annie said brightly. "I was afraid inventorying those storage units might take me forever. The less I have to worry with, the better! Sammy, you've been a big help. I really appreciate all your cooperation."

"That's no problem, Miss Annie. Let me know if I can be of any help to you."

Annie walked back to the porch and called to the Frisbee players on the front lawn, "Come on in, gang! We've got work to do!"

Annie was rummaging through the file cabinets when the Frisbee team poured through the door with Pixie leading the way. "Whatcha doin', Annie?" Lisa asked as she gently tugged at the Frisbee Pixie was still carrying in her mouth.

Annie closed one drawer and opened another and without looking up, said, "I'm looking for lumber invoices."

"Fourth cabinet from the left, bottom drawer in the back," Lisa said. Annie turned and glared at her. "What's the matter? I organized them while we were looking through all that stuff the other day. I didn't think they were important so I bundled them together and threw them all in one file. What's going on, anyway?"

Annie told Lisa, Barbara and Joe about her conversation with Sammy Dalton. Barbara came back from the kitchen with a beer in her hand and took a seat beside Joe and Lisa on the sofa. Barbara popped the top on the can and said, "I don't get it. How does Sammy fit into the picture?"

Annie located the lumber invoices where Lisa said she would find them and then took a seat in the armchair to look through them. "I think Sammy helped Tom Finley plan the fire at the factory. It's Insurance Fraud 101, and it goes something like this: Sammy and Tom take the lumber out of the factory, place it in Sammy's storage units, and then set the fire. Tom Finley tells his insurance company all the lumber was destroyed in the fire, and the insurance company pays him for it. Then, when all the commotion is over and everything settles down, Tom and Sammy sell the lumber at market price and split the take. They get paid twice for the same lumber, and no one is ever the wiser."

"But why would Sammy tell you there isn't much lumber left in the storage units?" Barbara asked.

"Because after tonight, there won't be. Sammy is going to incriminate himself when he moves the lumber....tonight. Without Tom Finley, Sammy can't collect his share of the fraudulent insurance claim. So, he's decided he'll cut his losses, sell the lumber and keep all the money for himself. He still makes quite a nice little chunk o'change."

"How do you know he won't move the lumber at the Knoxville location first instead of the Pigeon Forge facility?

"Because I told him we are going to begin taking inventory of the units at the Pigeon Forge location tomorrow morning and that we won't get to the Knoxville units until sometime next week. He thinks he has some time to get the Knoxville units emptied, but he knows he has only tonight to remove the lumber from the Pigeon Forge units. And when he does, the police will be waiting for him."

At nightfall, Lisa parked the rented black truck a few hundred yards from the entrance to Sammy's Self-Storage and cut the engine. Annie turned on the interior light, opened the glove box and removed a pair of binoculars. Lisa asked, "Where'd you get those?"

"Sporting goods store," Annie said.

Lisa chuckled, "I hate to tell you this, Annie, but binoculars don't work at night."

"Night vision binoculars do," Annie replied coolly.

Lisa raised her eyebrows. "Well, pardon me!" she said, and then she winked at Annie. "You know how to work those things?"

"Sure," Annie said.

Lisa sipped coffee from a thermos, turned on the radio and searched for a country station, careful to keep the volume low, while Annie stared at the entrance to the storage facility through the binoculars.

After about two hours, a car pulled up to the entrance. "Here we go," Annie said. "Right on schedule." She watched as Sammy Dalton got out of the car and unlocked the gate. Soon a convoy of tractor trailers rolled up, and a small band of men and forklifts emptied the units, loading one truck after another. As each truck was filled, it pulled away and drove off into the night. Sammy left just ahead of the last truck, and Annie and Lisa followed them to a Knoxville warehouse where the unloading was already underway. Annie opened her cell phone and placed a call to the Knoxville police. "Yes, I'd like to report a robbery in progress." She provided the warehouse address to the dispatcher, and within ten minutes, three police cars were racing toward them with lights flashing and sirens blaring.

It was after 1:00 a.m. when Annie and Lisa made it back to the house. Barbara and Joe were at the kitchen table playing poker using nickels and pennies for chips. "You two should have seen the look on Sammy Dalton's face when those police cars rolled up and the cops ordered him and his drivers to lie down on the ground!" Lisa exclaimed. "Then Annie got out of the truck and started waving those lumber invoices at him! It was a riot!"

Barbara laid her cards on the table. "A pair o' kings," she said to Joe and then turned to Lisa, "What were you doin' while all this was goin' on?"

"I was just watchin' all the action from the truck."

"Three fives," Joe said to Barbara laying his cards on the table and sweeping a pile of pennies and nickels toward him. "So, did they arrest all of them?"

"They did," Annie said. "And now this crime fighter is tired. I'm going to bed."

"Mind if I play a few hands with Barbara and Joe?" Lisa asked as she took a seat at the table.

"Not at all," Annie said, kissing her on the forehead. "Well, goodnight everybody." Annie smiled when she heard the three of them laughing in the kitchen as she trudged upstairs to bed.

A nnie woke up the next morning with a throbbing head and a sore throat. Lisa sat down on the edge of the bed and shook down a thermometer she had found in the medicine cabinet. She rolled it gently back and forth between her thumb and index finger and read it before putting it in Annie's mouth. "Here, put this under your tongue," she directed.

"I'm telling you I don't have a fever! I'm not sick!" Annie objected, her words garbled by the glass stick now protruding from her mouth.

"Then why is your skin clammy and your throat sore?" Lisa said as she got up from the bed and went to look for some aspirin. "Not to mention those black circles under your eyes," she called from the adjacent bathroom. Knowing it was pointless to argue further, Annie conceded defeat, sighed and fell back against her pillow. She picked up the remote control, turned on the television and began surfing the channels. Soon Lisa emerged from the bathroom with a handful of bottles which she placed on the nightstand and then retrieved the thermometer from Annie's mouth. Annie waited for the verdict. "One hundred one," Lisa announced. "You see, I told you so." Lisa opened a couple of the bottles on the nightstand, poured a few pills into her hand and handed them to Annie with a glass of water.

"Whatever," Annie mumbled. She found Channel 7 with the remote, sipped at the cup of hot tea with honey that Lisa had brought her from the kitchen, and settled back to watch the morning news.

Lisa went back to the bathroom. Running a hairbrush through her silky brown hair, she peeked around the corner of the bathroom. "Joe's going to look after you today.

102

Says he's making you some kind of Navajo cold remedy or something."

"Where are you going?" Annie inquired. "I'll go with you."

"You'll do no such thing, Annie Proudfoot. *You* are going to stay in this bed and get well while *I* am going to begin the search for Julie."

"And just how do you propose to do that?" Annie asked.

"Lisa Cannon, investigative journalist, never reveals her methods. Not to worry, Annie. I promise I'll be careful. I'm just doing some research today."

"Where's Barbara?" Annie persisted. "What's she doing today?"

"Barbara is on a stake-out today," Lisa said casually.

Annie sat up in bed and cried, "What do you mean, Barbara's on a stake-out?"

Lisa fished a leather belt through the belt loops of her blue jeans. "I paid for a room in the hotel across the street from Flo Wilkerson's fleabag hotel in Knoxville. I gave Barbara your night binoculars and she's going to watch who comes and goes, you know, try to get some sense of what's going on there." Annie thought this was a good idea, but she wasn't about to admit it to Lisa. "Now, stay in bed and listen to Joe," Lisa said as she bent down, kissed Annie on the forehead, and turned off the lamp on the nightstand. "I'll be back this evening."

"Yes, mother," Annie replied. She fell back again on the pillows and picked up the remote.

"Cute, very cute," Lisa said. She blew Annie another kiss and closed the bedroom door behind her.

Annie watched Channel 7 News for about an hour, hoping there might be some coverage of Sammy Dalton's arrest in Knoxville the night before. Disappointed the story apparently would not receive any coverage, she was about to turn off the television and get some sleep when Jason Sowers' fresh face appeared on the screen. He was updating his viewers on the Finley murder investigation. Jason's close-up quickly disappeared when the camera angle shifted, revealing that the young reporter was standing in front of Sammy Dalton's insurance office.

"Local insurance agent Sammy Dalton was arrested late last night on multiple charges including larceny and receiving and transporting stolen goods. Dalton is alleged to have taken lumber belonging to Finley Furniture and valued at more than a quarter of a million dollars. The lumber was stored at Dalton's self-storage facility here in Pigeon Forge, and Dalton was arrested after allegedly transporting all of it to a warehouse in Knoxville late last night. Dalton was arraigned early this morning and is currently free on a one hundred thousand dollar bond. However, authorities now say that Dalton is a person of interest in the death of furniture manufacturer Tom Finley. Investigators believe Finley's death may have been related to an alleged insurance fraud conspiracy involving the suspected arson of the landmark Finley Furniture factory on Wednesday. Less than one week later, Thomas Finley was found dead at his Knoxville home, the apparent victim of a homicide. We'll have more on this story as it develops. This is Jason Sowers reporting for Channel 7 News."

Annie pressed a button on the remote and the screen went dark. She smiled, turned over on her side, and fell asleep.

Annie was awakened by the sound of the telephone. She glanced at the digital clock on the nightstand and read the glowing red numbers: 2:48. Annie picked up the handset and in a hoarse voice, managed a painful "Hello."

"Hello, this is Stephen Finley calling for Annie Proudfoot."

"Speaking," she said.

"Ms. Proudfoot, I am the son and sole heir of Thomas Finley. I'm calling first to thank you. I was given your name by Knoxville police. They said that you are responsible for recovering the factory lumber."

"Happy I could help, Mr. Finley," Annie said.

"Please, call me Steve. Secondly," he continued, "I am calling to find out what happened to the lumber in the Knoxville storage units. Police went there this morning, based on the information you gave them last night, and all of those units are empty. Did you ever actually see any lumber in those units or did you just presume they were full as well?"

Annie's head was still throbbing, and she was trying to understand what Steve Finley was telling her. "Mr. Finley, uh, Steve, you'll have to forgive me. I've come down with a flu virus, and my head is a bit muddy. Are you saying the Knoxville units are empty?"

"Yes, ma'am, that's what I'm saying."

"Well, they were full of lumber, just like the Pigeon Forge units. My grandfather and I checked them out ourselves only a couple of days ago." She took a sip of water from the nightstand to ease her throat.

"Well, they're empty now," Steve said. "I realize you had nothing to do with this; I just wanted to make sure you had verified they were full."

"Yes, absolutely. I saw it with my own eyes," Annie said. "Maybe Dalton cleared them out, but I think that's unlikely. I deliberately told him only yesterday that I wouldn't have the chance to inventory the Knoxville units until next week, but that I was going to inventory the Pigeon Forge units today. I wanted to be sure he emptied the Pigeon Forge location last night so that we could catch him red-handed."

Steve laughed, "You know, I didn't realize we had such a highly-trained inventory specialist on the Finley payroll."

"Sorry about that," Annie said sheepishly and then explained how she had become involved in the investigation. "We'll need to arrange for the return of all the company files to you." They agreed they should meet to discuss the case and exchange information relating to the investigation. "Would you be free for dinner on Thursday evening?"

"Absolutely!" Steve exclaimed. They made arrangements to meet at a local restaurant, exchanged pleasantries and hung up.

Annie had no sooner returned the handset to its place on the phone base when it rang again. She picked it up and heard an excited voice on the other end of the line. "Annie, this is Barbara!"

"Barbara, what's wrong? Where are you?"

"Whattsa matter with your voice? Ya sound like a bullfrog, honey! Hey, guess what?" Barbara asked without giving Annie the chance to answer her. "You will never in a million years guess who I just saw go into Flo Wilkerson's motel room!

"I'm not good at guessing, Barbara," Annie said holding her aching head.

"Sammy Dalton!"

"You're kidding!" Annie exclaimed. "Say, how did you know it was him? You haven't even met Sammy, have you?"

"No," Barbara said, "but the dumb ass has his name painted big as life on the side of his vehicle!" Annie remembered seeing "Sammy Dalton Insurance" on the car that had pulled up to the entrance of the storage facility the night before. "He's a big, burly guy, right? Beard, beer belly?"

Annie laughed out loud, "Yeah, that's him all right!"

"Well, I bought this little disposable camera at the convenience store next door. Snapped a picture of the son of a bitch going in and one of him coming out. Looked like he was lovin' up on Flo pretty good there, if ya know what I mean!"

"You're a gem, Barbara! An absolute gem!" Annie couldn't believe the words that had just escaped her lips, or the fondness she heard in her own voice for this woman whom she had despised only two weeks earlier. "Come on back here, girl! Looks like you got what you went there to get!"

Lisa came home around 6:00 p.m. to find Annie curled up on the sofa. Joe sat on the edge of the sofa spooning some herbal remedy into Annie's mouth. He had spent most of the day preparing what was obviously a bitter concoction and was busy assuring Annie it would cure whatever ailed her. Annie swallowed a tablespoon of Joe's potion and shuddered. "Where have you been?" she asked picking up a glass of ice water to clean her mouth of the taste.

"Nowhere important," Lisa announced as she walked to the sofa and laid her wrist on Annie's forehead. "Good, your fever's down."

Annie looked over at Barbara who had seated herself in the armchair to enjoy the show. "Go ahead and tell her," Annie said.

"Tell me what?" Lisa said, taking a seat at the end of the sofa and putting Annie's feet on her lap.

Barbara looked like a child whose teacher had just given her the floor during show-and-tell. "I took photos of Sammy Dalton visiting the hotel room of Flo Wilkerson," she said.

"What?" The shock on Lisa's face was obvious. "Are you certain?"

Barbara handed her a packet of photos she had had developed at a drugstore near the hotel. Lisa opened the packet and glanced at the photos one at a time. She stopped when she came to one that showed Flo standing in the doorway of her motel room with her arms wrapped around the neck of a husky, bearded man whose belly overhung the belt of his trousers. Lisa shook her head in disbelief, returned the photos to the paper sleeve from which she had taken them, and handed the packet back to Barbara.

"Any dinner left?" Lisa asked. Barbara sat there looking disappointed her photos hadn't gotten more of a reaction from Lisa.

"Plate's warm in the oven for you," Joe answered while guiding another tablespoon of his homemade tonic into Annie's mouth.

"Yuck! Thanks, Joe, but I can't stomach any more medicine," Annie said as she threw back the blanket that covered her and followed Lisa into the kitchen. Joe put the spoon into the bowl, set it on the coffee table and turned on the television to give Annie and Lisa the privacy they needed to talk. "Lisa, what's wrong?" Annie asked.

"Nothing," Lisa said, painfully aware that her tone already had made a liar of her.

"Now I know something's wrong, so you may as well spill it!"

Lisa put a quilted mitt on her hand, reached into the oven and pulled out the plate of food Joe had kept warm for her. "I can't talk about it in front of Barbara," she whispered. "Let's wait until we go upstairs."

"Oh, okay," Annie said. She retrieved a can of soda from the refrigerator, set it down in front of Lisa, and took a seat at the table beside her.

Lisa finished her dinner, and she and Annie decided to turn in early. Annie called to Pixie to follow them. Reluctant to miss any action that might occur downstairs and unaccustomed to going to bed early, the dog whined and curled up on top of Joe's feet in the living room. "Suit yourself," Annie said as she started up the stairs.

Annie collapsed on top of the comforter that covered the bed where she had lain for most of the day. She smelled the fresh scent of fabric softener on the pillowcase covers that told her Joe had not only made their bed, but he had also changed the sheets. Lisa brushed her teeth, slipped into her nightshirt, pulled the covers down and crawled into bed beside Annie.

"Ooooohh, Annie," Lisa groaned, "remind me to thank Joe for putting fresh sheets on the bed."

The two women lay there savoring the crisp clean feel of cotton against skin. "I think he ironed them," Annie said. "I know he irons the sheets at home."

"You know I love you, Annie," Lisa chuckled, "but if that is a hint, I don't do windows and I certainly don't iron bed sheets."

"No, I wasn't hinting," Annie said, snuggling close to Lisa, nestling her head into her lover's outstretched arm.

"Feeling better?" Lisa asked.

"Not one hundred percent yet. I think it was just a twenty-four hour virus, maybe." They lay there in silence for a few moments before Annie spoke again, "Now that we're alone, you wanna tell me what you were whispering about in the kitchen?"

"Oh, it's nothing," Lisa said, "nothing important anyway."

Annie sensed that whatever Lisa had learned earlier in the day, she certainly wasn't ready to talk about it. "Okay," Annie said, "we can talk about it whenever you're ready."

"Thanks, babe." Lisa found Annie's lips in the darkness and kissed her deeply. Then, with Annie still lying close beside her, she rolled onto her side and fell asleep.

The next morning the two women were awakened by sound of heavy footsteps on the stairs followed by a loud knock on the door and Barbara's booming voice. "Wake up, you two lovebirds! Time to rise and shine! Can I come in?"

"Do we have a choice?" Lisa mumbled and then called out, "Yes, Barbara, you can come in!"

The door flew open, and Barbara walked in and bounced down hard on the foot of the bed, jostling Annie and Lisa who were still half asleep under the covers. "Guess where we're goin' today, gals!" Barbara could hardly contain her excitement.

Annie wiped the sleep from her eyes, and peered from beneath the comforter at the large, cheerful woman now seated at the foot of the bed. "We?" she asked, her voice still weak and gravelly.

"I'll bite," Lisa said. "Where are *we* going?"

"The Great Smokey Mountain Flea Market!" Barbara announced. After breakfast, of course. *Joe and I got biscuits bakin' in the oven right now!!*"

"All right, already!" Lisa said. She and Annie knew they wouldn't be able to decline the invitation from this grown woman who was behaving like a kid at Christmas. "We'll be right down. Just let us get showered and dressed, for Pete's sake!"

"Okay, but don't dilly-dally!" Barbara cautioned. "The good stuff gets sold early!"

"What time is it, anyway?" Annie asked.

"Oh, 'bout a quarter to seven," Barbara said as she headed out the door.

"A quarter to seven?" Annie yelled, but Barbara was already on the stairs.

"Come on, we might as well get up," Lisa said. "We won't have any peace until we go to the flea market with her."

Half an hour later, Lisa appeared in the kitchen, showered and dressed, and a few minutes later Annie joined her. Barbara and Joe were already at the table eating breakfast. Lisa plucked a biscuit from a basket covered by a linen cloth and asked, "Are you going with us today, Joe?"

"I wouldn't miss it," he said.

"What makes you want to go to a flea market, Barbara?" Annie foolishly held out a small sliver of hope that Barbara might realize she had no good reason for wanting to go and abandon her plans.

Barbara took a drink of coffee and washed down a mouthful of fried potatoes. "It's not just *any* flea market, Annie," she insisted. "This is the Great Smokey Mountain Flea Market! It's a huge place with lots of vendors! Lots of good stuff! Trust me, you're going to love it!"

When breakfast was finished, Barbara cleared the table and stacked the dishes in the sink, promising she would do them when they returned. They piled into the truck and set off for the flea market.

When they arrived, the marketplace was already in full swing. Lisa found a parking spot in a small lot adjacent to the main parking area, but before she had even set the parking brake, Barbara was out of the vehicle and haggling with vendors over the price of cheap knock-off merchandise spilling over the sides of the cardboard boxes that lined their tables. Annie touched Lisa's sleeve and said, "Get a load of Barbara! Just look at her! She looks like an old pro, doesn't she?"

Joe was only a few steps away looking through a rack of leather belts. Annie knew he was searching for a replacement of the well-worn strap fastened around his waist by the sterling and turquoise buckle he always wore.

Lisa unbuckled her seat belt and looked at Annie, "Well, what should we do first?"

"I dunno. You?"

"Let's look for some t-shirts," Lisa suggested. They approached the clothing racks of the first t-shirt vendor they came to and began searching through them. Lisa selected a black shirt with a picture of Elvis in a gold suit on the front and "50 Million Fans Can't Be Wrong" written on the back. Annie chose a white tank top with a picture of Larry the Cable Guy on the front and "Git-R-Done" on the back. While she had no idea who Larry was or what his slogan meant, her instincts told her that this Cable Guy's imperative was simply a distillation of her own plain-spoken, no-nonsense approach to life that she was finding refreshingly commonplace among the people of Tennessee.

Their shopping complete, Annie and Lisa sat down at a small café table to enjoy a snack of soft pretzels and lemonade. Then, relaxed and with a couple of hours left to kill, Annie thought she'd try again to find out what Lisa had learned the day before. "Ready to tell me what you found out about Julie?"

Lisa smiled and shook her head, "You never give up, do you, Annie? Yes, I suppose it's time I tell you. It's nothing definite, really. In fact, I have no idea what it means, but it troubles me for some reason." Annie was now leaning forward at the table listening intently. Lisa continued, "I thought it was odd that Julie used her credit card for the account she shares with Barbara, when she bought her lunch at the Cracker Barrel on the day she disappeared, but when she went into Dollywood and rented the locker, she didn't use the card. She must have paid cash to enter the park because no credit card charges from Dollywood appeared on the statement Barbara obtained from the credit card company. When we found Julie's rental car parked at Dollywood, and her backpack in the trunk, I thought at first maybe she had been abducted. Now I wonder if that's what she wanted us to think."

"What are you talking about, Lisa? Where are you going with this?" Annie sat there looking thoroughly confused.

Lisa decided she would get right to the point, "I had a friend of mine at my bank in Santa Rosa pull Julie's credit. Either Julie or someone posing as Julie applied for a credit card a few days after she disappeared. Whoever it was gave an address in Provincetown, Massachusetts." Lisa paused and gave Annie time to think about what she had told her.

Annie removed her elbows from the table and sat back in her metal chair. "Are you saying you think Julie just up and moved to P-town and is letting her partner, her family and friends assume she....?"

Before Annie could think of how to finish her sentence, Lisa interrupted her, "She left me a message in that locker, Annie. I haven't deciphered it yet, but for some reason, I think she wanted me to know she is alive and well. Trouble is, I also think that, for whatever reason, Julie wants Barbara and her parents to think she died or just disappeared."

"But why?" Annie asked. "Why would she want to let *you* know she's alive, but let Barbara think she just disappeared without a trace? Oh, Lisa, Julie's not in love with you, is she?"

Lisa laughed out loud. "No, Annie, Julie's not in love with me," she said firmly. "And before you ask, I am *not* in love with Julie. Are you crazy?"

"Boy, what a relief!" Annie sighed. "For a minute there, I was starting to worry."

Lisa reached for Annie's hand and clasped it in her own. "I love *you*, Annie. *Only* you. Don't ever forget that." Annie sat there mesmerized by the deep brown eyes gazing at her from the other side of the table. "Now come on! Let's go find your grandfather and that *crazy woman* from *Looziana*!"

On Thursday evening, Annie arrived ten minutes late for her dinner date with Stephen Finley, who was already seated at a corner table with a glass of white wine when she arrived. A slender man of average height, he was dressed in a pin-striped three-piece suit that looked like it had been tailored specifically for him. The stiff cuffs of his heavily starched white shirt emerged subtly from beneath the sleeves of his suit jacket to reveal a pair of stunning gold and diamond cufflinks that Annie guessed must have cost a small fortune. A well-groomed moustache and beard and his shiny bald head, gave him a look of distinction. He pushed his chair away and stood up to greet Annie as the waiter led her to his table. "Ms. Proudfoot, it's a pleasure to meet you.

"Pleased to meet you as well," she said. "Please accept my condolences over the loss of your father." Annie extended her hand expecting the usual business handshake, but instead, he took her hand in his and kissed it.

"May I say you're looking quite lovely this evening," he said. Annie fought the instinctual urge to roll her eyes. Then he held her chair as she sat down.

Annie sensed Stephen Finley had more than business in mind, and she hoped to put a stop to his advances. "Uh, thank you. Mr. Finley," she began, "I'm afraid I have another appointment at nine, a scheduling mix-up, so I suppose we should get right down to business."

"Oh, very well," he said. "I took the liberty of ordering for you. I'm told the chicken marsala is excellent here." *A womanizing control freak*, she thought. Finley nodded at the waiter who, right on cue, approached and poured a glass of wine from the bottle already on the table. He set it before Annie. "This really is an excellent Chardonnay," he said lifting his glass and rolling the glass to savor the bouquet.

"Thank you," Annie said. She deliberately refrained from picking up her glass for fear Finley might propose a toast. "Where would you like for me to have the file cabinets delivered?"

"My, you *are* all business, aren't you?" he chuckled. "Very well, then." He returned his glass to the table. "Ms. Proudfoot, I'll get right to the point. I am a very busy man. Most of my time is devoted to the management of my law firm. I am very appreciative of your efforts in uncovering assets stolen from my father's business. And it appears you have also led the police to his killer. You are obviously a highly intelligent, capable woman, and I would like for you to assist me in settling the insurance claim for the business and disposing of any remaining assets of Finley Furniture."

"You know, I really appreciate the offer, but I have a funeral home to manage and...."

Annie was trying to think of how she should end her sentence when Finley interrupted her. "No, no, I simply won't take no for an answer."

"No, really." Annie continued, "Mr. Finley, I'm just here on vacation. Even if I wanted to...."

"I'll pay you five hundred thousand dollars," he said.

"Five hundred thousand dollars?" Annie's jaw dropped. "Mr. Finley, your father's company was.....how should I say this, uh...?"

"Failing?" Finley said, "Bankrupt? Washed up? How's that?" He smiled and sipped his wine.

"You know that Finley Furniture was in financial trouble?" Annie asked. She knew she couldn't erase the shocked look on her face.

"Of course, I know," he said expressionless. "I've known for years. In fact, it wasn't just in financial trouble; it was on the verge of total collapse." He smiled broadly. "That fire couldn't have come at a more convenient time."

Hmm, he's actually happy the factory burned, she thought. "But," she objected, "why would you want to pay me half a million dollars to liquidate a company that will most likely have a negative net worth when all is said and done?"

"Because I can, of course," he replied, as if the answer were obvious. "Honestly, I don't wish to deal with any of this. The family furniture business is nothing more than a headache for me, something I don't wish to deal with. You will have complete discretion. Now surely you can get someone to handle your funeral business for a couple of months. It really shouldn't take any longer than that. I'm sure it wouldn't even require you to stay here in Tennessee the whole time. You can travel back and forth as needed. You'll also have a generous expense account in addition to your compensation."

The waiter arrived with the chicken marsala. "Well, Mr. Finley," Annie said lifting her glass in a toast, "you've made me an offer I'd be a fool to refuse. I'll require half now, half when the liquidation is complete."

"Superb! Call my office in the morning, and my assistant will arrange for the transfer of funds. And I suppose this means you'll be keeping those file cabinets for a while."

"Thank you, Mr. Finley. I look forward to working with you."

The two finished dinner and shook hands outside in front of the restaurant to seal the agreement. Annie drove back to the house wondering how she was going to explain this to Lisa, Joe and Barbara.

It was dark when Annie's truck pulled into the driveway. Joe turned on the front porch light and pushed open the screen door to let Pixie out to greet her. Annie walked across the lawn and trudged up the porch stairs with the dog leading the way. "So how did the meeting go?" Joe asked. He held the door for his granddaughter.

"Oh, fine, I suppose," she said. "I just agreed to handle the insurance claim for Finley Furniture and the liquidation of the company."

Lisa, who was seated on the sofa watching TV with Barbara, jumped up when she heard Annie's words. "You did what?" she asked her eyes open wide. "Why on earth would you agree to such a thing?"

"He's paying me five hundred thousand dollars, Lisa. I couldn't pass it up."

"Five - hundred - thousand - dollars?" Lisa could not believe it. "How can a company on the verge of bankruptcy pay you a half a million dollars for its own liquidation?"

"Finley Furniture isn't paying me," Annie said. "Stephen Finley is." She paused and thought for a few moments. "I know, I know, it makes no sense. Still, it's a bundle of money! I just couldn't turn it down. Besides, it's a great opportunity to learn more about what was going on at Finley just prior to the fire. It might help us figure out who killed Tom Finley."

"Annie, I thought that was settled. The police have fingered Sammy Dalton for the murder."

"Maybe. I guess I'm not as sure about that now," Annie said. "I mean, if Tom Finley and Sammy Dalton were conspiring to defraud the insurance company by moving the lumber and then setting the fire, then Sammy probably stood to gain a lot more from his share of the insurance settlement than he would have gotten just from the sale of the lumber. With Tom Finley dead, Sammy couldn't collect any of the insurance money. So Sammy would have had no obvious motive to kill Tom, unless, of course, they had some sort of disagreement."

"Well, let's think about who else might have had reason to kill him."

"What about Flo?" Barbara said without taking her eyes off the television. Annie, Lisa and Joe looked at each other and then at Barbara. "After all, she worked at that factory for more than thirty years. If I's employed by someone for that long, and I suddenly found out my retirement and savings had been messed with, I'd wanna kill the no-good bastard who took my money, that's for sure! She was still talkin' about it on the way to Knoxville the other day. I couldn't believe it. We had just told her that her husband is dead, and her daughter is missing, and that woman is worried about her retirement money!"

"I doubt she would be capable of murder, Barbara," Lisa said.

"All of us are capable of killin' somebody, Lisa," Barbara countered. "Under the right circumstances, every person on this planet is capable of murder."

"But Tom Finley was strangled with a rope," Annie said. "I doubt a woman would have the upper body strength to subdue and kill a man that way."

"Maybe," Barbara said. "I just think we should keep Flo on the radar, that's all. After all, who woulda thought she was havin' an affair with Sammy Dalton?"

"Who else might have had reason to kill him?" Joe asked.

"Stephen Finley," Annie said. Lisa, Joe and Barbara just looked at her. "You heard me. I think Stephen Finley may have killed him."

"But why? What reason would he have had to kill his own father?" Lisa asked.

"I dunno. I have no particular reason to suspect him. It's just a feeling I have, that's all. He seemed not the least bit concerned over his father's death. He never mentioned it during dinner. He just knows he has a mess to deal with at Finley Furniture, and he wants me to take care of it. He also smiled and said the fire couldn't have come at a more convenient time. It was like he was happy the place was destroyed."

"Anyone else we should add to the list of possible suspects?" Joe asked.

"Who knows what kinds of shady deals Tom Finley might have been involved in," Lisa said.

"Or what shady characters he was friends with," Barbara added.

The next day Annie called Stephen Finley's office to arrange for the funds transfer of half of the compensation they had agreed upon. She used a fax machine to obtain the paperwork authorizing her to settle the insurance claim on behalf of Finley Furniture and to liquidate any remaining company assets. Annie hoped that, when all was said and done, there might be at least some money left to reimburse the employees' retirement and 401k plans.

When this was done, she got into the truck and drove to Sammy Dalton's insurance office. The receptionist greeted her as she walked in. "You must be Tabitha," Annie said. "You probably don't remember me, but we spoke on the phone a few days ago. I'm Annie Proudfoot. I'm afraid I don't have an appointment, but I really need to speak with Sammy Dalton."

A look of fear settled on Tabitha's face. "Yes, uh, yes, I remember quite well." Tabitha recognized Annie as the woman responsible for her boss's current legal difficulties. Tabitha's voice suddenly took on a sharp tone, "I'm afraid Mr. Dalton isn't seeing anyone at this time."

"I'll just be a minute," Annie said and sidestepping Tabitha, she opened Sammy's office door and stepped inside.

Tabitha was right behind her. "I'm sorry, Mr. Dalton. I tried to tell her you aren't seeing anyone, but she just walked in anyway and...."

"It's all right, Tabitha," said the large man behind the desk. "Just close the door on your way out." He motioned for his secretary to leave them alone. "Sit down, Ms. Proudfoot," he directed. Annie took a seat in front of his desk.

"I realize this is awkward," she began, "but...."

"Awkward?" he roared. "You're damn right it's awkward! You come here to Tennessee from God knows where, stick your nose where it doesn't belong and in just one day you manage to ruin my marriage, my business, my whole life. Lady, I'll be lucky if I don't spend the rest of my life in prison because of you! Now, what in the hell do you want from me?"

Annie leaned forward in her chair and looked Sammy Dalton straight in the eye, "I want you to tell me what the arrangement was between you and Tom Finley."

Sammy laughed, "Lady, you've got some nerve, I'll give you that! Do you honestly think I'm going to give you the rope so you can hang me with it?"

"Sammy," Annie said, "you are a thief, but I doubt you're a murderer. I don't think you killed Tom Finley, but the police are already working hard to pin his death on you. And I'll work just as hard to prove you are innocent of his murder as I did to prove you were guilty of theft."

Sammy sat there in silence for a few moments considering Annie's offer. "Oh, what the hell! I have very little left to lose because of you, and it's all gonna come out eventually. You wanna know what Tom and I were doing? Well, I'll tell you! Tom and I were friends since high school, so when he took over the family business, he purchased insurance from me. A few months ago, Tom came to me with some serious problems. His company was failing. He had no more credit, and the business his grandfather started back in 1927 was just about to collapse. Tom asked me if I would help him out, so I agreed to store the lumber from the factory. He was going to set the factory on fire, tell the insurance company that the lumber was destroyed in the fire and claim it in the insurance settlement. Then he was going to remove the lumber from the storage units and sell it. Tom had already emptied the employees' retirement fund and 401k plan just to keep the business going. He thought that burning the factory down was the only way. Tom felt he had no choice but to toss a match to it all, and I know it was wrong, but Tom's been a good friend to me over the years and I honestly just wanted to help him out. I wasn't going to make one red cent on this deal! And now, just look at what I'm going to get for trying to help a friend out!"

Annie sat there shell-shocked. "Sammy, if you didn't stand to profit, why did you move the lumber to Knoxville?"

"After Tom was murdered," Sammy continued, "everything changed. I knew that if the lumber turned up, the money from its sale would go right into Stephen's pockets, and Tom's employees wouldn't get a dime! I thought if I could keep Stephen from finding out about it, if I could keep it all outta his hands, I could sell it and send the money to the Finley Furniture employees. That's the way Tom woulda wanted it."

"Oh, Sammy! I'm so sorry!" Annie exclaimed. "If I had only known...."

"Anything else you wanna know?" Sammy asked. Impatient, he tapped the eraser of a pencil on the desk

"Yes," she said. "I want to know who killed Tom Finley. Any thoughts?"

Sammy shook his head. "No, I'm afraid I don't," he said curtly, "now if you'll excuse me." Annie knew this was her cue to leave. She got up, went to the door and looked back at Sammy, who just stood there staring at her. She wanted to apologize but was unable to come up with the right words, so she said nothing and closed the door behind her.

When Annie returned from her visit with Sammy Dalton, the garage door of the Wilkerson house was up and Lisa, Joe and Barbara were busy carrying dozens of white plastic bags from the trunk of Flo's old brown car into the house. Annie pulled the truck into the space beside Flo's car and rolled down the passenger side window as Lisa grabbed three bags in each hand. "I don't want to hear it, Annie," Lisa protested before Annie could say a word. "If we're going to be here another two months, we need groceries and supplies."

"Hello to you, too, sweetheart," Annie said laughing.

"Sorry," Lisa said. "I thought you were about to give your *'Lisa, we don't need all this stuff'* speech."

Barbara put down a handful of bags on the kitchen table and returned to the garage for more. "Annie," she said, "you got a call today from some insurance lady. Said she's handling the Finley claim. Steve Finley's office gave her your number. She wants you to call her when you get a chance. Her number's on the pad beside the phone."

"Okay, thanks, Barbara," Annie said peering into a couple of the remaining bags in the trunk. "So, what's for dinner?" Lisa glared at her, and then, without saying a word, she picked up the last of the groceries and walked into the house. "What? What'd I say? I just asked what we're having for dinner."

"Pizza," Joe said. "Delivery," he added for clarification so that Annie wouldn't make the mistake of asking how long it would take Lisa to make it.

Annie walked into the living room while Barbara and Lisa emptied the bags and put the groceries away. She tore the top page from the notepad beside the phone and dialed the number. The phone rang, and a woman answered, "Hello, this is Ivy Peterson. How may I help you?"

Annie read the name on the paper and determined this was the woman whose call she was returning. "Ivy, this is Annie Proudfoot returning your call. I assume this is about the Finley claim."

"Oh, yes," Ivy said, "thanks for getting back to me. Stephen Finley advised me you will be handling the claim on his behalf."

"Yes, that's correct," Annie said.

"I was wondering if we could arrange a meeting to discuss the claim process," Ivy said.

"Certainly," Annie replied, "the sooner the better."

"How about tomorrow?" Ivy suggested.

"Perfect," Annie said. The women agreed to meet at the Wilkerson house the following morning. "I'll have some coffee and donuts ready."

Annie hung up the phone and walked into the kitchen. Cans and boxes were lined up on the counter beside the sink. Annie knew they had been placed there because there was no more room in any of the cabinets, and she silently congratulated herself that she knew better than to mention this to Lisa. "Good news! Looks like this Finley job might be moving faster than I thought," she announced. "At this rate, we could be home in time for Christmas!"

At this, Lisa got up from the table, opened the door and said, "I think I left something in the car." She stepped into the garage and slammed the kitchen door behind her.

"I don't understand," Annie said exasperated. "I thought she'd be happy about it."

Joe shook his head. He wondered if Annie would ever learn how to read the moods and unspoken signals of the woman she loved.

When dinner was over, Barbara and Joe sat down to play a few hands of poker, and Annie and Lisa retreated to their bedroom without speaking.

Lisa changed into her pajamas, brushed her teeth, got into bed and turned onto her side so that she lay facing the wall. Annie sat down on her side of the bed and began untying her shoes. Uncomfortable with the silence between them, she decided she would be the first to break the silence. "I just don't understand what you're angry about, Lisa," she said looking over her shoulder. "I'm making good money on this job, and it may help us find out who killed Tom Finley. Who knows, it may even lead us to Julie!"

Lisa rolled over on her back and stared at the ceiling. Annie could see the tears streaming from the corners of her eyes and running down her cheeks. "I guess I just wanted us to spend the holidays together, the two of us, alone. At home, for heaven's sake! I just wish you had talked to me before making the decision for all of us to stay here another two months."

Annie was stopped short. She suddenly realized that her unilateral decision to accept Stephen Finley's offer of employment had been made without regard to Lisa. She had foolishly assumed Lisa would just happily go along with whatever she wanted. Annie rolled onto the bed beside Lisa, propped herself on one elbow and with her free hand gently brushed the tears from Lisa's face. "I'm sorry, Lisa. I'm really sorry. I thought I was making a decision that was best for us, but I guess, in reality, it was just best for me. I promise, from now on we'll make these kinds of decisions together. Promise."

Lisa managed a smile, lifted her head from the pillow and kissed Annie lightly on the lips. "Don't make promises you can't keep, Annie Proudfoot!"

"And," Annie paused, "if you want me to tell Stephen Finley I can't do the job after all, I will. Then we'll pack up and fly back to Santa Rosa. We could leave as early as tomorrow." Annie drew a breath and waited for Lisa's answer.

Lisa sat up in bed indignant, "And waste all those groceries and supplies I spent the whole afternoon shopping for? Are you crazy?" Then her expression and her voice softened, "No, we'll stay here in Tennessee until you're finished. Just being with you, Annie, is really all that matters to me." She paused for a moment, and Annie got up and started toward the bath. "So, Annie," Lisa called to her from the bed, "will you be with me? Be with me now, Annie." The seduction that filled her voice and eyes was unmistakable. Annie turned around and started back toward the bed as Lisa lay down again on the pillow and slowly unbuttoned her own satin nightshirt. "Of course, you know, don't you," her voice took on a lusty tone as she slid her arms from the sleeves, "there are times when I *want* you to make decisions for me, times when I *want* you to tell me what you want me to do? And this is one of those times, Annie."

Annie stood there mesmerized by Lisa, who she realized was teasing her. In one quick motion, Annie pulled her shirt off over her head like a ball player stripping off a warm-up jacket. Then she unfastened and removed her bra, freeing her small, firm breasts that were already anticipating the pleasure they were about to encounter. Annie stood there in only her blue jeans and belt and watched as Lisa slowly parted her own legs and let her long fingers wander through the wet stream that flowed deep

133

inside a mound of thick, dark hair and pink flesh. Her hips now undulating, Lisa moaned as she pleasured herself, her fingers moving in a rhythmic, pulsing motion. Then, postponing her own climax, Lisa lifted her wet hand from its task, and, turning it so that her palm was up, she brought her index finger toward her palm, beckoning Annie closer. "Be with me now, Annie," she said again, her voice thick with desire, "and tell me what you want me to do." She wondered how long Annie could contain her own passion, and the tension of restraint excited both of them all the more.

Annie unzipped her jeans and stepped out of them easily as she moved closer toward the summoning finger which, when it reached Annie's face, traced its wetness on her lips. She smelled and tasted her lover's sweet, heady scent, and licking the wetness from Lisa's hand, Annie savored the sticky sweetness that covered each finger.
.
In an instant Annie was straddling Lisa, fondling her full breasts and gazing into her deep brown eyes. A surge of power coursed through Annie's body, a bolt of lightning that left her only with an urge to dominate this woman whose body lay writhing beneath her. Annie hovered close to her lover's face and whispered in her ear, "I just want you to let me do whatever I want." She kissed her neck and sucked her breasts. Licking taut nipples, she held them gently between her teeth, pulling and releasing them like a hungry calf seeking milk from its mother's teat. Annie moved lower until she was seated between Lisa's legs now spread wide, a banquet awaiting one guest. Hands grasping buttocks lifted the luscious fruit to her mouth. Annie burrowed her face into soft, thick hair and lapped juice from the cleft of the peach until her tongue found the pink budding flower it was seeking. She ate until both she and Lisa were satisfied, then she kissed Lisa on the mouth so

that she might taste her own sweet wetness. When their passion was fully spent, they fell asleep exhausted, still wrapped in each other's arms.

The next morning Ivy Peterson arrived on time for her appointment with Annie who greeted her at the front door and welcomed her into the house. Ivy was a tall, slender black woman dressed in a plum-colored skirt and jacket with a purse and heels to match. Her hair was pulled back tight into a bun which sat atop her head like a crown, and a gold necklace and earrings contrasted beautifully against her smooth dark skin. In her right hand she carried a fine leather briefcase. "May I get you a cup of coffee?" Annie said as they walked through the living room to the kitchen.

The smell of fresh-brewed coffee had drifted through the screen door and reached Ivy's nostrils before she had stepped inside and she was glad that Annie had made her the offer so quickly. "I'd love it!" Ivy exclaimed.

"Please, have a seat and make yourself comfortable," Annie said. "Cream or sugar?"

"Thanks," Ivy replied as she took a seat and set the briefcase on the table. "Just a small splash of cream, please." She opened the case and took out a stack of papers as Annie set a porcelain saucer and coffee cup on the table next to her.

"Donut?" Annie opened the Krispy Kreme donuts Lisa had purchased at the grocery store the day before. She held the box in front of Ivy for her to make a selection.

"No, thank you," Ivy said. "They look delicious, but I'm trying to watch my weight." She then retrieved a pair of reading glasses from the briefcase and turned her attention to the stack of paperwork in front of her as Annie returned to the table with her cup of coffee.

"Stephen Finley's office faxed me the paperwork yesterday authorizing you to handle the claim on behalf of Finley Furniture, Inc. I've reviewed the authorization and everything appears in order. Despite the ongoing investigation concerning the death of Tom Finley, our company is prepared to proceed with settlement of the claim." Confused about why the murder investigation had any bearing on the insurance claim for the factory fire, Annie looked at her quizzically. "I just need your signature here," she said pointing to a place on the document, "and here, and once more on the last page." Ivy had highlighted the areas requiring Annie's signature.

She handed the paperwork to Annie, who sat quietly reviewing the documents while Ivy drank her coffee. Confused, Annie quickly laid the papers on the table, looked at Ivy and said, "Ms. Peterson, these documents have nothing to do with the claim for the fire at the factory."

"Why, of course not!" Ivy said. "I'm here to settle Thomas Finley's life insurance claim."

"I'm afraid there's been a mix-up," Annie said. "I thought you were here to discuss the factory claim."

"Oh, there's no mix-up, Ms. Proudfoot. This document clearly authorizes you to handle the life insurance claim. You see, as President and Chief Executive Officer, Mr. Finley wanted to make sure that, in the event of his death, the company would have the funds it needed to carry on without him. Finley Furniture, Inc. is the owner of the policy, as well as the beneficiary. You see?" Ivy said, handing her the signed authorization.

Annie hadn't bothered to read the authorization when Finley's office had faxed it to her, so she took the form from Ivy and read it thoroughly for the first time. She quickly discovered that it was a loosely worded authorization giving her almost total authority to handle any and all claims involving the Estate of Thomas Finley. It looked like a boilerplate form taken straight from a legal textbook. *For an attorney*, she thought, *Stephen Finley didn't prepare a very well-defined document.*

If Ivy Peterson was satisfied Annie had the authority to settle Tom Finley's life insurance claim, Annie decided she would just play along. "What is the face value of the policy?" she said as she signed the documents in the spaces Ivy Peterson had highlighted.

"Ten million dollars," Ivy said unphased as she wrote out the draft, signed it and handed it to Annie, who read it aloud: Annie Proudfoot, on behalf of Finley Furniture, Inc.

That's one hell of a motive for murder, Annie thought as she took the draft from Ivy and laid it on the table in front of her.

Stephen Finley walked past his secretary and into his office. His secretary Doris didn't even take her eyes off the computer screen as he passed by since he didn't customarily greet her on his way in. He had barely closed his office door when she heard his voice on the intercom, "Doris, hold all my calls."

Doris pressed the button on the intercom to answer him, "Yes, Mr. Finley." Disgusted, she released the button and returned to her work, mumbling under her breath, "I'd hold all your calls, you old goat, if you ever had any calls to begin with!"

Doris Campbell had worked for Stephen Finley's law practice for only two months, but she had worked as a legal secretary for more than forty years. Following her retirement from a large Knoxville law firm, she had grown bored and had answered a newspaper ad placed by Stephen Finley. It had taken just two days for her to discover that despite his pretentious manner, Stephen Finley was a miserable failure as an attorney. He had only a handful of clients, whose cases he was busy fumbling. Over the years Doris Campbell had worked with her share of incompetent lawyers, but none quite so inept as Stephen Finley. She was looking for other employment to fill her time, but had decided that, in the meantime, she would stay on with Finley if only to enjoy the spectacle of his incompetence.

Within ten minutes, he was on the intercom again: "Doris, get Fidelity Life Insurance on the phone for me."

She located a letter in her in-basket with Fidelity's number on it and placed the call. Once Finley was on the line, she hung up the phone. She looked up to see Annie Proudfoot coming through the door. "Good morning," Annie said, checking the name plate on the desk, "Doris. My name is

Annie Proudfoot. I'm handling the Finley Furniture claims for Stephen Finley."

"Yes, yes," Doris said with a smile, "I believe we spoke on the phone day before yesterday. Won't you sit down?"

"Thank you," Annie said cheerfully. "I'm afraid I don't have an appointment, but was wondering if Mr. Finley might have a few moments to speak with me."

"I'm sure he can spare the time," Doris said. She picked up the handset on the intercom and informed Finley that Annie was there to see him. "You can go right in," she said to Annie, nodding in the direction of Finley's office.

Annie stood up to go in when Stephen Finley threw open his office door and emerged to bark again at Doris. His face, ears and bald head were tomato red and Annie half-expected steam to rush from his ears at any moment. "Doris, call those bastards at Fidelity again and get the claim representative's name and number. I need to get Dad's life insurance claim settled and they keep putting me on hold."

Annie interrupted, "That won't be necessary, Doris. I met with the claim representative yesterday and have already settled the life insurance claim." Doris swallowed what otherwise would have been a hearty laugh when she saw Finley's face turn white as a sheet and he looked as if he were about to pass out. Unflinching, Annie turned to Finley, "Mr. Finley, may I have just a few minutes of your time."

Finley held the door and nodded for Annie to enter. "Please, sit down," he said pointing to one of two leather office chairs in front of his executive desk. "So, you say you settled my father's life insurance claim?" he asked. Annie could tell he was trying hard to maintain his composure, but she could tell Stephen Finley was clearly confused about how she had become involved in the life insurance claim.

"Yes," she replied,. "I was contacted by an insurance representative, who I assumed was contacting me about the claim for the factory fire. She said your office referred her to me."

Finley looked as if he was about to have a stroke. "So, uh, where's the check?"

"Excuse me?" Annie said.

"Where's the check? The life insurance check?" Finley was growing impatient.

"Oh, I deposited it this morning," Annie said casually.

"You what?" Finley exclaimed nearly coming up out of his seat. "How did you deposit it? Wasn't the check made payable to me?"

"No," Annie said. "Actually, I was as surprised as you seem to be. Turns out, your father's life insurance was purchased by Finley Furniture. The company is both the owner of the policy *and* the beneficiary. I deposited the life insurance proceeds in a trust account until we can get a handle on the company's financial situation.

Finley looked as if he were going to be sick. "Oh," he managed, "I guess I misunderstood. My father just told me he had ten million dollars of life insurance. Since I am his only heir, I just assumed I was the beneficiary on the policy."

"Well, if your father owned all the shares of corporate stock, you'll get whatever is left after the company's debts and obligations are paid. I can check on that if you like," she offered.

"Uh, okay," Finley said. "I think he did own all the stock." A little bit of color returned to his face when he realized he might get some of the insurance money after all.

"Obviously," Annie continued, "we won't know anything until we determine how much debt the company had." Finley shifted again in his seat. Amused by her newfound ability to make him squirm, Annie decided that while she had his rapt attention, she would give him one more cause for concern. "And, of course, the top priority will be to re-fund the company's retirement and 401k plans. I don't know if you're aware of this, but your father misappropriated those funds to keep the company afloat." Now the small amount of color that had briefly returned to Stephen Finley's face drained away again. "Well, I know you're a busy man, so I won't take up any more of your time." Annie got up to leave. "I just wanted to keep you informed."

"Uh, I appreciate that, Annie. I really do," he said. He opened the door for Annie and found Doris Campbell standing at the doorway.

Offering a quick response, Doris said, "I was just getting ready to knock, Mr. Finley."

Annie suspected Doris was lying, and when Doris flashed half a wink her way, Annie knew she had been listening at the door. Quickly resuming her professional manner, Doris said, "Ms. Proudfoot, I have a file from the fire insurance company that I would like to review with you sometime, paperwork you'll want to look at before meeting with the insurance representative."

"Sure, Ms. Campbell," Annie said, "why don't we do it now? I'll take you to lunch."

"Please, call me Doris," she said.

"Okay, Doris," Annie said, "are you free for lunch?"

"I sure am," Doris said, "Just let me grab the file and my purse and we'll be on our way."

Annie pushed open the glass door bearing Stephen Finley's name in gold letters, and held it open as Doris walked out ahead of her. "There's a little diner just down the street, if that's all right with you," Doris suggested.

"Perfect," Annie said. "So, how long have you worked for Mr. Finley?"

"Only two months, but before that, I worked as a legal secretary for one of the bigger firms here in Knoxville for forty years," Doris said. "I retired last year, but within a month I was bored, so I decided I'd go back to work."

"How long has Mr. Finley been in practice?" Annie asked, hoping to get Doris to open up.

"Ten years," Doris said, "but just between you and me, the man probably doesn't know any more today than he did the day he graduated from law school, which wasn't much to begin with. I'll bet you think I'm terrible for talking trash about my boss, don't you?"

Annie laughed, "No, no, I don't. I got the impression he's having a little trouble understanding the situation with his father's insurance."

"I'll let you in on a little secret," Doris chuckled. "You know that authorization form you signed? Steve printed it from a CD of fill-in-the-blank legal forms he bought at Staples. He didn't even edit it! It's a catch-all form, so loosely worded it might even authorize you to have him committed to an asylum for all he knows! And if you ask me, that's where the fool belongs!"

"Sounds like you don't like your job," Annie observed as they walked toward the restaurant.

"He doesn't have enough cases to keep *himself* busy, let alone a full-time secretary. And he doesn't even know what to do with the ones he has! I'm looking for another job right now. I'm really just putting in time until I find something else."

"Well, how does he make a living if he has only a few cases?" Annie asked.

Doris lit up a cigarette as the two of them walked along. "Stephen's lived off his father's money his whole miserable life. He was a professional student for over ten years. First, the old man paid to put him through college, then law school, and finally, he put him on salary at the furniture factory. Steve was supposedly counsel for Finley Furniture, but the truth of the matter is that the company didn't require much in the way of legal counsel. I think it was just an excuse for Tom Finley to keep forking money over to his no-good son. If you ask me, I think his father was in denial about the fact that his son is a loser."

They arrived at the diner, and Annie opened the door for Doris, who threw her cigarette on the sidewalk and stomped on it with her heel before going in. When they were seated at a booth, Annie looked over the top of the menu at Doris and asked, "What's in that file anyway?"

"Oh, it's a just proof-of-claim form the insurance company sent to us," Doris said dismissively. "To tell you the truth, I just made up all that about needing to discuss the file with you. I really just wanted a chance to talk with you alone and let you know what kind of a man you're working for!"

Annie shook her head and laughed, "So, tell me what's good to eat here, Doris!"

After lunch with Doris Campbell, Annie drove to the Knoxville Police Department to speak to the officer in charge of the Finley murder investigation. She was directed to Detective Cassandra Belton, a twenty year veteran of the Knoxville police force. "Just call me Cass," she said as she shook Annie's hand. Calloused hands, broad shoulders and a straightforward manner made Annie wonder whether this tall woman with short red hair and freckles had grown up on some nearby Tennessee farm. "The case is obviously still open, but to be honest with you, Annie, we really don't have any promising leads. I wish I could tell you more, but I'm not really supposed to be discussing the investigation with anyone."

"Sure, I understand," Annie said. She told Cass of the information she had found concerning Finley Furniture and suggested there might be something in the filing cabinets at the Wilkerson house that could help Cass with the murder investigation. "If you like, I'd be happy to let you take a look at the files."

"Gee, that'd be great!" Appreciative of Annie's willingness to show her the files, Cass then said, "Hey, can I buy you a cup of coffee?"

"Sure!" Annie said, "I never turn down coffee." Over a cappuccino and conversation at Starbucks, Annie decided she would take a chance. "You know, you're probably going to think I'm crazy. But I have a friend I think you might hit it off with, and ...."

"I'd love to," Cass replied smiling.

"What?" Annie said.

"I said I'd love to," she said again. "You were going to ask me to have dinner with y'all, weren't you?"

"Well, yes," Annie said surprised Cass had so quickly anticipated her question.

"Okay, it's settled. You say when and I'll make sure I'm there. Maybe we can talk some more about Tom Finley then, too."

"Well," Annie paused, "that's great! We'll see you on Saturday around four o'clock?"

"I'll be there!" Cass exclaimed.

When Annie got back to the house, she tossed her keys on the kitchen table where Lisa was working on some files. Then she walked to the refrigerator and opened the door to search for a snack. "Hmmm, chocolate pudding," she said, pulling one of the plastic pudding cups from a box and peeling the top back.

"Don't spoil your dinner," Lisa scolded without looking up from her file. Annie took a spoon from the silverware drawer, scooped some pudding out of the cup and, flying it through the air as she made airplane sounds, she guided it to Lisa's lips. Lisa swallowed the pudding and raised her eyebrows, "Hmmm."

Annie followed the spoonful of pudding with a soft brief kiss. "Good, huh?"

"Which?" Lisa asked. "The pudding or the kiss?" Lisa asked.

"Either or both," Annie said.

Lisa let her hand hover above the table, tilted it left and right like a plane banking its wings and wrinkled her brow. "Aaahhh, so-so I guess," she said. "I've had better." She waited a few seconds before glancing up from her papers and smiled coyly. "You know I'm just kidding, don't you, Annie?"

"Too late," Annie said. "You'll get no more from me."

"Pudding or kisses?"

"Either," Annie smiled. "So, what are you working on there?"

"Oh, it's just some of my notes on Julie. I just don't understand what could have happened to her. I mean, we know she was in Pigeon Forge on the day she disappeared. If she called Flo Wednesday morning to say she wasn't coming, why did she fly here, have lunch at Cracker Barrel and leave a rental car at Dollywood? Then, she leaves a cryptic message in a locker and vanishes into thin air. None of it makes any sense."

"Any more activity on her credit report?" Annie asked while scraping the sides of the pudding cup.

"Nothing. The trail is completely cold."

"Well, why don't you fly up to Massachusetts next week, you know, to the address provided by whoever applied for credit in her name last week."

"What good would that do?" Lisa looked completely dejected. "I mean, if Julie *is* alive, certainly she would have been in touch with us by now. Maybe she went to the factory to see her father and both of them died in the fire."

"I guess it's possible," Annie said still scraping the inside of the plastic cup furiously with the spoon.

"Do you think you've gotten it all yet?" Lisa asked. "For heaven's sake, Annie, get another one! There's a whole box of 'em in the fridge!"

"My, we're touchy, now aren't we?" Annie said tossing the empty pudding cup into the trash can. "Go ahead and fly to Massachusetts, Lisa. You won't get any rest until you do."

"Do you think I should take Barbara along?"

"I wouldn't," Annie said with no sign of doubt in her voice.

"Why?" Lisa asked. "After all, Julie is *her* partner."

"I wouldn't because you don't know what you may find. Suppose you find her alive. I'm afraid it would only hurt Barbara. If Julie is living in Massachusetts, maybe she doesn't want to be found."

"What are you saying?" Lisa closed the file folder and propped her elbows on the table, her head in her hands.

"I'm saying that if Julie ran off, for whatever reason, it might be better, less painful, if we let Barbara continue to believe she's dead."

"Do you honestly think the woman just ran off with no explanation at all?"

"I don't know," Annie said. "Right now, I don't know what to think. You fly to Massachusetts and see what you can find out, and I'll tell Barbara you've been called away to interview someone for a magazine article."

"Okay," Lisa agreed. "I'll call the airline."

Joe decided he would give the four women the chance to get to know each other, and so on Saturday afternoon, he drove Flo's old brown car to the casino in Maggie Valley to spend the day with some one-arm bandits.

The doorbell rang at quarter to four and Barbara jumped up from the sofa to answer the door. "You must be Cass! I'm Barbara Thibodeaux. Pleased to meet ya!" Barbara stuck out her hand and shook Cass's.

"Pretty strong grip you got there," Cass said. She picked up a brown grocery bag by her feet and stepped inside.

"Uh, Annie and Lisa are in the kitchen," Barbara said, pointing the way. Barbara returned to the sofa and picked up the remote. She turned the volume down on the latest fight that was breaking out on the Jerry Springer show she and Joe had taped earlier in the week.

Cass walked behind the sofa carrying her brown bag and stopped to watch the brawl. "I love this show," she said. "I didn't know it was on Saturdays."

"It's not," Barbara said. "I just tape the weekday shows to watch on the weekends."

Annie walked into the living room from the kitchen wiping her hands on a tea towel. "I thought I heard the doorbell. Glad you could make it, Cass," Annie said taking the brown bag from her arms.

"Uh, thanks," Cass said barely glancing away from the screen. "There's, uh, a bottle of wine and a six pack of Bud Light in there."

"Now, the man on the left," Barbara pointed to a man with a ponytail on the TV screen, "he left his wife, the skinny one there with the short hair, for that trailer trash in the halter top." Suddenly, a fight broke out between the two women on the television screen, and bouncers were trying to separate them amid all the scratching and clawing. Barbara and Cass broke out in loud laughter. Barbara turned around, reached into the bag Cass had handed to Annie, and pulled out two long neck bottles. She handed one to Cass, who quickly took a seat on the sofa beside her. They twisted off the bottle caps almost simultaneously and settled in to enjoy the show.

Annie shook her head and walked back into the kitchen where Lisa was removing a casserole from the oven. "So what's going on in there?"

Annie smiled, "Well, it looks like we have another Jerry Springer fan. Barbara's bringing Cass up to speed on the action."

Lisa removed her oven mitts, walked into the living room and introduced herself to Cass. "Dinner will be about another ten minutes, you two," she said to the women on the sofa whose mumbling confirmed for Lisa they had heard her.

Lisa walked back into the kitchen, where Annie was sipping a glass of wine and flipping through the pages of a magazine on the table.

"Can you believe those two?" Lisa said in disbelief.

"I'm glad they're getting along so well. Maybe striking up a friendship with Cass will get Barbara's mind off Julie for a bit. I had a feeling they'd hit it off!"

Soon the four women sat down to dinner and Cass kicked off the conversation. "So what brought y'all here to Tennessee?"

"It was supposed to be a vacation but it turned into a disaster en route." Lisa feigned a smile, "Please pass the butter, Annie."

"You see," Annie continued, "we got off the plane in Knoxville and stopped at this little diner where we learned that the Finley Furniture factory had burned."

Barbara jumped in, "Annie, you forgot to tell her about Julie. My partner Julie was supposed to pick us up at the airport but she never showed up."

The women spent most of dinner bringing their guest up to speed on their time in Tennessee. "Sounds like y'all need some help out here. "Well, you got the right woman now," Cass said lifting her beer from the table and toasting the others.

"Uh," Annie began, but Cass interrupted her.

"Now there's no need to thank me, Annie."

"But I wasn't...." Annie tried again.

"No, I'm here and happy to help y'all!" Cass exclaimed. "Sounds to me like you need someone with law enforcement experience to make some headway on this investigation."

"Well, we certainly appreciate that but we know you're a busy woman." Annie knew it was useless to object.

"Now, Annie," Cass continued, "I won't take 'no' for an answer. Yes, I'm busy, but I always make time for my friends."

Barbara raised her bottle of beer toward Cass. "I think it's just great that Cass is willin' to help us out. You know, Annie, you've been doin' a good job, but we can use all the help we can get."

"Well, then, I guess that's settled," Annie said swilling the wine that remained in her glass. She heard the defeat in her own voice and hoped no one else did. But Lisa had heard it loud and clear and although she wanted to soothe Annie's wounded ego, she knew it would have to wait until they were alone.

The conversation for the rest of the evening was lively. Barbara boasted of her sexual exploits with Julie and half the women in Louisiana while Cass bragged about her adventures as a Knoxville police detective. Annie remained downstairs until ten o'clock to dispel any notion that she had been wounded by Cass's hijacking the investigation. Then she retreated to the upstairs bedroom while Barbara and Cass continued their endless chatter. Soon Lisa excused herself as well, and went upstairs to find Annie lying quietly in the darkness. Lisa didn't say a word, but crawled into bed beside Annie and held her gently in her arms until both of them fell asleep.

After a couple of hours, the voices downstairs faded away and the house was silent. Joe came in late to find the lights out and everyone asleep. On the sofa lay a tall redheaded woman he didn't recognize. He walked quietly down the hall to his bedroom and closed the door.

Cass Belton was awakened the next morning by what felt like a wet piece of sandpaper on her cheek. She opened her eyes to find herself looking into the soulful eyes of a Golden Retriever panting eagerly and pawing at her arm for attention. "Pixie!" Cass heard a loud whisper. "Pixie, come!" Soon Cass saw a silver-haired Navajo man standing over her. "Go back to sleep. I'm sorry she disturbed you," he said quietly. Joe pulled on Pixie's collar to coax her away from the sleeping woman who readily closed her eyes again.

When breakfast was ready, Joe led Pixie to the bottom of the stairs. "Go get 'em, girl. Wake 'em up!" Pixie bounded up the stairs and pushed open the door to Annie and Lisa's room with her wet nose. She leaped onto the bed and collapsed between Annie and Lisa, barking and pawing first at one and then the other.

"What is it, girl?" Annie asked in a sleepy voice and then she heard Joe's voice at the bottom of the stairs.

"Annie, Lisa, breakfast is ready."

He walked down the hall, knocked at Barbara's door and called her to breakfast. Joe then went to the sofa and extended his hand to the redheaded woman who was now awake, sitting up and holding her head in her hands. "Hi, I'm Joe Proudfoot, Annie's grandfather."

"Cass Belton," she said shaking his hand. "Pleased to meet ya!"

"Hangover?" Joe noticed a coffee table littered with empty beer bottles.

" Yep," she admitted.

Joe walked to the kitchen and returned with a glass of tomato juice. "Here, drink this."

"Thanks!" Cass drank it down, fumbled for her boots at the end of the sofa and began lacing them up. "I can't believe I overslept," she said. "I'm gonna be late for work."

"You work on Sunday?" Joe asked.

"Sure do," Cass said. "I'm a police detective."

"Won't you stay for breakfast?"

"I'd love to, but I can't," she said as she found her jacket and slipped into it. She picked up her wallet and keys from the coffee table, shoved them into her pocket and started for the door just as Annie and Lisa were coming down the stairs with Pixie leading the way. "Annie, Lisa, thanks for everything! I'll be in touch with you in the next day or so." Cass tousled the hair on Pixie's head and was out the door and down the porch steps. A few seconds later, they heard her fire up the engine of the unmarked police cruiser and head off down the road.

"Thank the Lord, she's finally gone," Annie muttered to herself. She yawned and poured a cup of coffee for herself and one for Lisa.

"Who was that woman, Annie?" Joe asked.

"Cass Belton, police detective for the City of Knoxville," Annie said plainly. "She's in charge of the Finley murder investigation. I made the mistake of contacting her and now she's ready to take over. She says we need help from professional law enforcement, and, miracle of miracles, she's willing to help us out!"

Sensing Annie's anger and looking for guidance, Joe glanced at Lisa who shook her head slightly to indicate he should not pursue the issue further. Joe knew Lisa would fill him in later, so he thought he'd change the subject. "So where do we go from here?"

"Tomorrow morning, I'm flying to Massachusetts to look for Julie," Lisa said, "but as far as Barbara is concerned, I'm on assignment for a magazine article."

Joe persisted, "Okay, Annie, how about you, me and Barbara? What's the game plan?"

"I'm meeting the Fire Marshal and the insurance representative tomorrow morning," Annie said. "I think I'll ask Barbara to follow Stephen Finley just to make sure he's not up to something we don't know about, and, Joe, why don't you pay Flo Wilkerson a visit? She seemed to like you. And she obviously knows more than she's telling."

"Annie, what should I say to her when she asks how we found her?" Joe asked as he walked to the stove and removed a plate of hotcakes from the oven.

Annie thought for a moment and said, "How about something like this: *Flo, we thought you were lying to us about visiting your sister so we followed you from the airport and it turns out we were right, you **were** lying.*"

Barbara staggered into the kitchen holding her head as Annie and Lisa were sitting down at the table. "Barbara, you're just in time for breakfast," Joe said. "How 'bout a plate of hotcakes and some coffee?"

"No thanks," Barbara said reaching into the refrigerator and pulling out a can of beer. "I had one too many last night. Time to fight fire with fire, and my head is definitely on fire." She cracked open the can and took a drink. "You gals want one? It'll cure whatever ails ya!"

"No thanks," Lisa said laughing.

"None for me, thanks," Annie said.

"Hey, am I glad you met Cass! I gotta hand it to you, Annie, she is one hell of a woman! We talked until two in the mornin'. You know, I really think she's gonna be able to help us out, don't you? That's what I like about you, Annie. If you can't get the job done yourself, you sure as hell know how to find someone who can!" Barbara threw her head back and finished off the beer as Annie's face flushed red and she started to come up out of her seat.

"Easy girl," Lisa muttered quietly as she grabbed Annie's leg under the table and pulled her back down into her seat.

"Yeah," Barbara continued, "she and I are gonna work on the investigation together. I'm meeting her this morning. I think she's gonna be able to help me find Julie, and maybe she'll even solve that Finley murder, too! Who knows! Anyhow, Annie, I can't thank y'nough."

"But ...," Annie objected.

"Sorry, Annie, gotta run! I'm meetin' Cass over in Knoxville this morning. She's gonna gimme some training on surveillance techniques." Barbara tossed her empty beer can in the garbage can and headed back the hall toward her bedroom. "I'll take Flo's ol' clunker so you can have the truck," she called to Annie just before she slammed her bedroom door behind her.

"Gee, thanks. Imagine that, I get to drive the truck that *I'm* paying to rent." Annie picked at the hotcakes on her plate with a fork and then put it down on the plate. "Surveillance techniques? Is she serious?" Annie looked at Lisa who simply shrugged her shoulders. "Well, Joe, looks like you're on double duty tomorrow. How about tailing Stephen Finley after your date with Flo Wilkerson?"

"You got it," Joe said. "Now finish your breakfast."

While Annie went to meet the insurance claim representative about the factory fire, Lisa and Joe took a taxi to the Knoxville airport. Joe carried Lisa's bags into the terminal and saw her to the gate. "Be careful, and call us when you get in," he said putting the bags down. He kissed her on the cheek.

"Thanks, Joe," Lisa said as she took a seat to wait for her flight. "Now don't worry about me. I'm fine. Just keep an eye on Annie. In case you didn't notice at breakfast this morning, she's not really happy about Cass Belton's involvement, especially when Cass and Barbara tramp all over her ego."

"Oh, I noticed all right," Joe laughed. "I thought she was gonna come right across the table at Barbara this morning. Don't worry, Lisa, I'll keep a check on her."

Joe walked from the gate to the rental car counter inside the terminal. From there he walked to the rental lot, jingling a set of car keys in his hand. When he reached the lot, he matched the numbers on the keychain to the parking space numbers in the lot. "Oh, no," he sighed when he spied the car he had been assigned. He fired up the car and headed for Flo Wilkerson's motel.

It was about noon when he pulled into the space in front of Flo's room. He shoved the car keys into the front pocket of his jeans as he walked to the door. Joe knocked, but there was no answer, so he knocked again. About to return to his car, he noticed a maid pushing a cart toward the door. "Ms. Wilkerson in?" she asked Joe in broken English.

"No answer," Joe said stepping back to make room for her cart.

The maid pulled the cart in front of Flo's door, retrieved a heavy key ring from her pocket, and unlocked the door. Joe had returned to the car and was preparing to drive away when the maid ran from the room screaming, her hands over her eyes. "Miss Flo, she is dead!" she said. "So much blood!"

Joe pulled the cell phone from his belt and called 911. Then he walked inside to see for himself what had become of Flo Wilkerson. He found her in the bathroom, naked in a tub full of red water, the inside of both arms slashed deep from the wrist all the way to the elbow. On the closed toilet seat was a half empty glass of rum and coke poured from bottles on the sink counter. The smell of alcohol mingled with the metallic smell of blood filled Joe's nostrils, leaving him nauseated. Seeking some fresh air, he turned to leave and ran smack into the same tall redheaded woman whom he had seen sleeping on the sofa the morning before. She was standing in the doorway to the bathroom, her thumbs tucked into the belt loops of her trousers.

"Fancy meetin' you here, Joe!" Cass said. "Hm," she gruffed, "they said this might be a homicide. Looks more like a suicide to me."

Annie drove up to the charred remains of the furniture factory and got out. A man with a clipboard hanging from his belt was running a tape measure around the footprint of the building. Annie leaned against the bed of the truck and waited for him to finish. Her cell phone rang.

"Annie, it's Joe. I drove here to see Flo like you asked me and...." He paused.

"And what?" Annie extended her hand to the man with the clipboard now walking toward her.

"She's dead. Flo is dead," Joe said.

"Annie Proudfoot, pleased to meet you."

"What?" Joe said.

"Excuse me just one moment," she said to the claim adjuster. "I'm sorry, Joe. I'm out here with the insurance guy. How did Flo die?"

"She's in the bathtub of her motel room with her wrists slit. It's a gruesome sight."

"Suicide?" Annie asked.

"Well, that's what Cass thinks, but I'm not so sure." There was silence on the other end. "Annie, you still there?"

"Yes, Joe, I'm still here," Annie said. "Did you just say Cass thinks it's a suicide?" Not waiting for him to answer, she kept going, her voice escalating, "What in the hell is Cass Belton doing there?"

"She's a homicide detective, Annie. It's her job."

Annie agreed that they would continue their discussion at home. Joe ended the call, returned the phone to the clip on his belt and stepped back inside Flo's room to let Cass know he was leaving when he heard a familiar voice behind him. "Well, I'll be damned! What are you doin' here Joe?" He turned to see Barbara standing in the doorway with a cardboard carrier filled with coffee cups. "Coffee?" Joe accepted one of the Styrofoam cups from the carrier. Just then, Cass Belton came up to them dangling a plastic baggie with something shiny in the bottom. "What zat?" Barbara asked handing Cass a cup of coffee.

"It's a diamond cufflink. Found it under the bed. Looks like Flo had herself a gentleman caller," Cass concluded.

L eaning across the passenger seat of a rental car, Lisa strained to see the house numbers on the proud Victorians lining the street of the old neighborhood. She glanced again at the address on Julie Wilkerson's credit report to make sure she was looking for the right number: 9435 Regency Row. Her car drifted slowly beneath a quickly thinning canopy of sugar maples which had laid down a welcome mat of orange and gold confetti on the street. Lisa tried to imagine what the pastel painted ladies might have looked like when they were first built at the turn of the century, long before these now *old broads* received their facelifts from urban yuppies with a penchant for nostalgia.

She pulled up in front of a three-story home whose soft pink exterior glowed in the late afternoon sun. Satisfied she had the right address, she parked at the curb and made her way up the walk. A tired cream-colored Mercedes bearing a handicapped tag was parked in the driveway. Surface rust in the wheel wells betrayed the car's otherwise well-cared-for condition and told Lisa it was at least twenty years old. Hanging baskets of brightly colored fall flowers lined the wraparound porch which had been freshly painted white. She surveyed the well-manicured lawn and shrubbery, admiring flower beds of marigolds and chrysanthemums of white and orange and purple.

Lisa walked up the wooden steps and onto the porch and rang the bell. While she waited, she glanced at the black mailbox next to the door where a handful of white envelopes stood like folds of a clean handkerchief from the breast pocket of a suit jacket. She read the name on the address label of one of the envelopes just as the elderly woman who lived in the house peered through the leaded glass of the heavy wooden door.

The door opened and there stood an elegant older woman in a neatly tailored pants suit. She stood tall and ram rod straight, though she leaned on a fine hardwood cane crowned with a scrolled silver ball that Lisa guessed was solid sterling. The fingers of the strong hand that gripped it were long and tapered, glittering with mine-cut diamonds in art-deco platinum settings that matched her cropped silvery white hair. Like the exterior of the house she lived in, her smooth complexion and finely chiseled features concealed her age, and she exuded a sensuality that intrigued her younger visitor. Her face and manner were stern, yet Lisa knew that beneath this mask, this elderly woman was much like herself: a woman who loved women.

Remembering the name on the white envelope, Lisa blurted, "Yvonne Roberts?"

"Yes," she replied, reluctant to volunteer more information. She paused, wondering what the young woman standing before her would say next.

"Ms. Roberts," she began, "my name is Lisa Cannon. I am a friend of a young woman named Julie Wilkerson. I'm not sure how to explain this, but...."

The old woman turned on her cane to walk away, and Lisa feared she had made this trip for nothing, until the woman looked over her shoulder, smiled and called to her, "Come in, Ms. Cannon, I've been expecting you."

Lisa pulled open the screen door and followed the woman into a parlor where a silver tea service and fine porcelain teacups with gold rims and trimmed with roses rested on a tray on the coffee table. "Please, sit down," she said, referring Lisa to a camelback sofa while she sat down in a wing chair. She poured a cup of tea and handed it to Lisa.

165

"Julie has told me a lot about you. She thinks very highly of you, you know." She poured a second cup for herself and added, "And I can certainly see why."

Lisa fought the blush she knew was appearing in her cheeks and composed herself. "Have you seen Julie? Is she all right? We've been so worried about her. She's been missing and ..."

The older woman interrupted, "I'm afraid Julie is a very confused young woman."

"Are the two of you related?"

"Oh no, no, we're not related," she smiled. She placed her cup in the saucer, set it on the coffee table and sat back in her chair. "You see," she began, "I taught library science at Tulane for many years. I was Julie's advisor. She and I grew close because we obviously shared some of the same, shall we say, affinities."

"Affinities?" Lisa asked. She knew very well what Yvonne Roberts meant but wanted to make her voice it.

"Yes, we both love books and women, not necessarily in that order," she chuckled.

"Were you two involved romantically?" Lisa asked.

"Oh, no, we weren't. The attraction was there certainly. Well, it was for me, anyway, but I guess the timing just wasn't right. My partner Gwen was battling cancer at the time. She died the year after Julie graduated."

"I'm sorry," Lisa said.

"Well, thank you. Anyway," she paused, "by that time, Julie was already involved with that woman, you know, that Cajun from back in the swamps."

"You mean Barbara?" Lisa asked, displeased with the attitude of her hostess.

"Yes Bar-bar-a," she said sarcastically. "Truly a shame that that woman was Julie's first sexual encounter. You know, Ms. Cannon, first love is a very powerful thing and Julie quickly became invested in that uncouth brute of a woman, who I'm sure was neither romantic nor gentle with Julie." Ms. Roberts again leaned forward in her chair and returned to her tea. "Despite my pleading with her, she insisted on staying with that woman until...."

"Barbara," Lisa corrected.

"Yes, Barbara," she said, the impatience in her voice increasing. "I tried to get Julie to leave a long time ago, but she refused. I guess she finally had had enough."

"Are you saying that Julie suddenly just decided to disappear? Left Barbara without saying a word? With no explanation at all?" Lisa heard the disbelief in her own voice, which had jumped at least an octave.

Yvonne Roberts raised then lowered her eyebrows and smiled as she lifted the porcelain teacup to her lips once more. She made no answer and knew she didn't need to. In an instant Lisa had read the answer in the woman's face and suddenly felt an ache somewhere in her torso. She couldn't quite pinpoint its location, nor could she determine whether it was in her heart or her stomach since both were churning. A momentarily disorienting wave of sadness mixed with anger washed over her, and in her confusion about why Julie would do such a thing, Lisa blurted, "Well then, where is she?"

"She was here for the first few days," Yvonne replied dismissively, "but I can't tell you where she went after that?"

"Can't or won't?" Lisa snapped.

"Won't." Yvonne finished her cup of tea and placing it in its saucer, set it firmly on the coffee table.

Now angry, Lisa could feel her face begin to flush. She stood up, shoved her hand into her jeans pocket and pulled out a crumpled piece of paper which she threw into Yvonne's lap. "And just what is this all about?" she shouted. "Does Julie think this whole thing is some kind of game, some morbid joke? Or is she just so spineless that she lacks the common decency to let her partner and her friends know whether she's dead or alive?" Lisa fought the urge to cry not just for the worry they had endured over Julie's disappearance, but also for the heartbreak Julie apparently had been so willing to inflict on Barbara.

Yvonne picked up the creased paper and read what was written on it: LLC-GO-2-AL-C724.112. "I think this is a message for you," she said flippantly.

"Fine," Lisa said. "Now tell me what it means! Why does she think I'm interested in playing her stupid little games?"

"Look," Yvonne said, "Julie just couldn't face that woman and tell her she was leaving her. Personally, I don't know why she gave a damn, but Julie is soft-hearted. She didn't want to hurt anyone so she decided it would be much easier just to let that Cajun woman think she had been killed or abducted. Julie wanted to make a clean break, you see. No crying, no pleading, no torturing herself with needless guilt over it all. We decided this was the best approach for everyone involved."

"Lady," Lisa shook her finger at her hostess and was preparing to unload on her when her cell phone rang. Excusing herself, she answered it and heard Joe's voice on the line. She stood there stone-faced as Joe conveyed his message, then she closed the phone and returned it to the clip on her belt.

"As for the message she left for you on this paper," Yvonne held the note aloft, "she's directing you to the Albuquerque Library."

"Whatever," Lisa said unconcerned. "Whenever you see Julie," she added, tell her that both her mother and father are dead. Her mother was just murdered in some cheap motel in Knoxville. Her father died in a factory fire. Tell her she can call me if she wants any of the details." Lisa ripped the wrinkled paper from the other woman's hand, walked to the door and slammed it behind her.

Lisa hurried down the walkway to her car. She slid into the driver's seat and, while buckling her seat belt, she glanced in her rear view mirror. She couldn't believe what she saw. She looked more intently at the person walking briskly along the sidewalk toward Yvonne Roberts' house. It was Julie Wilkerson! A small apricot poodle trotted ahead of her, its jeweled pink leash held firmly in her hand. Lisa's first instinct was to get out of the car to confront Julie, drag her by the ear into Yvonne Roberts' house and give them both a piece of her mind. Then she thought better of it and decided to let the opportunity pass. She reasoned that neither Julie Wilkerson nor Yvonne Roberts deserved even a moment more of her time, so she returned her gaze to the street up ahead. She started the car and drove away without looking back.

Lisa drove to the airport and caught the next flight back to Knoxville. When the plane was finally in the air, she reclined her seat, leaned her head back against the headrest and closed her eyes. She resolved not to tell Barbara about Julie, sparing her friend the pain and humiliation she knew such news would bring.

Joe pulled his new rental car into the garage. Annie had heard him coming and was standing in the doorway into the kitchen, a glass of iced tea in hand. "Eeewwww! Let me get my sunglasses!" she exclaimed laughing. "I know you, Joe. You rented a sunshine yellow car so Barbara wouldn't want to borrow it to practice her surveillance techniques, didn't you? And it's a convertible too!"

He laughed as he followed her into the kitchen. "Doesn't really blend in, does it?"

"Did Lisa catch her flight on time?" Annie began clearing the kitchen table of the insurance paperwork for Finley Furniture.

"Yes, the flight was right on schedule," Joe said. "I called her this afternoon to let her know that Flo's dead. She said she'll be flying in this evening."

"Does she want us to pick her up at the airport?"

"No, she's planning to rent a car and drive back here. I'm hoping they give her something to drive that isn't bright yellow, something I can use to tail Stephen Finley."

"So what conclusion has 'The Great Cass Belton' reached concerning Flo Wilkerson?" Annie held her hands aloft facetiously and improvised an exaggerated gesture when she spoke the name of this detective she had so quickly grown to detest.

Joe knew better than to admonish Annie when she was feeling so vulnerable. "Cass thinks Flo committed suicide," he said quietly, "which just goes to show she's not as great a detective as she thinks she is."

"What do you mean?" Annie asked, curious about what Joe might have observed in Flo's motel room.

Joe took a seat at the table. "Well, Flo had very deep lacerations from the wrist to the elbow of both arms. If it had been a suicide, she would never have been able to cut the other arm after slicing through the tendons and muscles in the first arm. Each of her arms was cut nearly all the way to the bone. And there would have been no need for her to cut the second arm anyway. Flo would have been losing blood so fast, it's doubtful she would have been able to maintain consciousness long enough to cut herself a second time. No, it was obviously staged to look like a suicide, and anyone with half a grain of sense should have seen that. Frankly, I was surprised that Cass bought into it so fast. No, there's no doubt about it, Annie, Flo Wilkerson was murdered."

"Hmm," Annie mused. "Did you notice anything else?" Annie was relieved to know that, even though Barbara had been won over quickly by Cass Belton's crowing, neither Joe nor Lisa would be so easily misled.

"Well, Cass did find a beautiful gold and diamond cufflink under the bed. I think it may belong to Flo's killer. Cass doesn't seem to think it's important at all. Oh, she thinks it might belong to Flo's lover, but she clearly doesn't intend to pursue it as a clue to the identity of her killer. Because, of course, Cass doesn't believe there *is* a killer."

"Was it a large diamond solitaire in a yellow gold setting?" Annie asked. "Like this?" She picked up a piece of scrap paper and a pen and drew a quick sketch of the impressive diamond cufflinks that Stephen Finley had worn to their first meeting.

"Yes," Joe said, "that looks like it exactly! How did you know?"

"Stephen Finley has a set of cufflinks just like that," Annie replied.

Just then Barbara burst through the front door, more excited than Annie or Joe had ever seen her. "Hey, you guys!" she yelled. "Get in here! You gotta see this! Cass and I's gonna be on the six o'clock news!"

In the time it took Annie and Joe to get up from the table and walk to the living room, Barbara had already leaped over the back of the sofa and grabbed the remote control from the coffee table. She was scrolling through the channels just as fast as her fingers could tap the buttons. When she came to the local news channel she had been searching for, she stopped and ran up the volume on the remote until the news anchor's voice was blaring and crackling through the television speakers. "Gosh, Barbara, we can hear it! Turn it down already!" Annie said putting the tips of her index fingers into her ears until the crackling and thumping coming from the speakers subsided. Then she sat down in the overstuffed chair while Joe took a seat beside Barbara on the sofa. News anchor Jason Sowers' segment was already underway.

"You see! You see!" Barbara cried, pointing at the screen. "There I am! There I am!"

Annie looked at Joe and rolled her eyes as Jason began to speak. "Police have identified the victim as Florence Wilkerson of Pigeon Forge. Knoxville police detective Cass Belton is investigating the death which is being treated as a homicide. Detective Belton is seen here taking

173

insurance agent Sammy Dalton into custody. According to Detective Belton, Mr. Dalton is being charged in the death of Flo Wilkerson which occurred just this morning at the Southern Comfort Motel in Knoxville.

Barbara's eyes remained glued to the television screen as the camera zoomed in on Cass Belton leading a cuffed and shamed Sammy Dalton from the door of his insurance office to the place where Jason Sowers was standing. Cass handed Sammy off to a uniformed officer and then walked up to Jason's microphone like a peacock preparing to spread its colorful plumage for the Channel 7 viewing audience. Like a drapery tieback, the hand on her hip held her jacket away from her waist to expose the shiny detective's badge clipped to her belt and the edge of the leather shoulder holster that held her service revolver.

"Isn't she just great?" Barbara exclaimed.

"Marvelous," Annie said flatly. She picked up her glass of ice tea from the coaster on the end table next to her chair and jiggled it so that the half-melted ice cubes tinkled against the sides of the glass.

"Sshhhh!" Barbara scolded her, taking the glass from Annie's hand and setting it on the coffee table. "I wanna hear this!" Then she used the remote to run up the volume on the television again.

Attempting to tune out the fiery redhead's bragging, Annie picked up a magazine and flipped through its pages until Jason Sowers finished his interview with the woman who was fast becoming Knoxville's hotshot detective. When the broadcast was over, Barbara pressed the power button on the remote causing the screen to go black. Then she leaned back on the sofa and propped her feet on the coffee table with her hands clasped behind her head.

Curious, Joe remarked, "Barbara, Cass told me this morning at the motel that she thought Flo's death was a suicide."

"Yeah, well, uh, at first she did," Barbara replied.

"What changed her mind?" he persisted.

Clearly pleased with herself, Barbara said proudly, "I did!"

"You?" Annie said.

"Well, don't look so surprised, Annie!" Barbara seemed offended by Annie's tone. "Cass says I have a good head for investigative work. I showed her the photos I took of Flo and Sammy. Then there was the cufflink. All of it points to Sammy."

Annie rolled her eyes, and decided to press Barbara further. "Just out of curiosity," she smiled, "how did Cass determine the cufflink in the motel room belongs to Sammy Dalton?" Joe looked at Annie warily; he knew this tone of voice nearly always backfired on her.

"Uh, well, uh, she hasn't....yet," Barbara stammered, "but I'm sure it's just a matter of time before she proves it belongs to Sammy."

Hoping she had sown some doubt about Cass's ability as a detective, Annie continued to spew her sarcasm, "Oh, of course."

The room fell silent for a few moments when they heard a key inserted in the front door made the doorknob rattle. Then the door opened and Lisa stood there looking exhausted.

"Hey everybody!" she called before realizing that Annie, Joe and Barbara were all seated in the living room, but everyone remained quiet. "Oh, there you guys are!" Lisa threw her backpack in the corner and collapsed into the armchair across from Annie. "Gosh, am I tired!" Still no one said a word, so Lisa decided she would make a point. "Hi, Lisa!" she continued. "How was your day? Fine, thanks for asking. What the heck is wrong with you guys?"

"Oh, Annie's just jealous that Cass has already solved Flo's murder," Barbara announced.

Annie stood up and exclaimed, "What!" But before she had even gotten to her feet, Barbara had gotten off the sofa and the two women began pointing in each other's face and shouting incoherently.

"Stop it, you two!" Lisa ordered but her voice couldn't be heard above the din. "I said, 'Stop it!'" Still the two women continued their shouting match. "I—Said—Stop!" she screamed in a shrill voice. Startled, Annie and Barbara stopped arguing and returned to their corners. Lisa sat back in her chair and looked at Joe, who sat quietly on the sofa.

Barbara stomped down the hall to her room. "I'm goin' to Cass's for a while!"

"Yeah? Well how are you gonna get there 'cause you're not taking the truck! Knoxville's a long walk from here, sister!" Annie called after her.

"Annie, that's enough!" Lisa said sharply.

Barbara stormed out of the room with a duffel bag and headed out the front door. "You can keep your damn truck, Annie. I'm takin' Flo's old car!" she said slamming the door behind her.

Annie stood up and started for the stairs. "I'm going to bed."

"But it's only 6:30," Lisa objected, but Annie was already on the stairs and didn't answer.

Lisa turned to Joe, "What in the hell happened here?"

He shook his head and then, with his hands on his thighs, he stood up and started toward the kitchen. "Come on," he said, "I'll explain everything to you over a bowl of ice cream."

Annie was up early the next morning. She fixed a pot of coffee and sat down at the kitchen table to resume her work on Finley's insurance claim. Lisa wandered into the kitchen around nine, but Annie didn't even look up from her work. Lisa poured herself a cup of coffee and kissed Annie on the top of the head before sitting down beside her.

"Joe already gone?" she asked, hoping to break through the shell that had formed around Annie the night before.

"Yes," Annie said coolly.

"He said he was going to get an early start," Lisa added. "Look, Annie," she continued, I'm sorry I was so sharp with you last night. It was a rough day yesterday, and I didn't expect to come back to a shouting match." Still Annie didn't respond. "Actually, I'm relieved that Barbara won't be here today. I was hoping to get the chance to talk with you alone."

"Why?" Annie asked.

"I found Julie Wilkerson in Provincetown."

Annie looked up, her eyes widening at the news. "She's alive then...?"

"Oh, yes, and living with her advisor from Tulane, an older woman named Yvonne Roberts. Apparently, Roberts had a thing for Julie at one time."

"Well, what did Julie have to say? Why did she just run off?"

"I didn't speak to Julie. In fact, she doesn't even know that I saw her. The Roberts woman lied to me. She told me she had seen Julie a few weeks ago, but that she didn't know where Julie had gone. Then, as I was preparing to drive away, I saw Julie in my rear view mirror. She was walking Roberts' poodle."

"Hm," Annie grunted, "Nothing surprises me anymore."

Lisa took a sip of coffee and then kept talking, hoping Annie's countenance would soften. "Yvonne Roberts said Julie just wanted to get away from Barbara and that the two of them, Julie and Yvonne, thought this was the best way to leave without hurting her. Can you believe that? I told Yvonne to tell Julie her parents are dead and that if she wants any of the details, she can contact us."

Annie made no response, and the room was silent except for the scribbling sound of her pencil lead on a yellow legal pad.

"I love you, Annie. You know that, don't you?"

"I'm angry, Lisa, but not with you," Annie said as she continued to scratch figures across the paper, pressing the mechanical pencil hard against the tablet. Lisa rose, moved behind Annie's chair, tightly wrapped her arms around Annie and kissed her gently on the back of the neck.

Annie laid down her pencil, leaned her head back against Lisa and closed her eyes, but like water that seeps through closed floodgates, an uneven stream of tears escaped from beneath her eyelids and ran quietly down her cheeks and onto Lisa's hands, which were clasped tightly around the woman she loved. "I love you, too, Lisa," she said.

By midday, Joe Proudfoot had followed Stephen Finley to a sleazy bar on the lower side of Knoxville, just a few blocks from the motel where Flo Wilkerson had met her untimely death just the day before. Finley pulled into an alley alongside the bar while Joe parked about a hundred yards away. It was only 11:00 a.m., but already the bar's patrons were flocking to the front door like faithful parishioners to church on a Sunday morning.

Joe went inside and took a seat at the bar with a good view of Stephen Finley, who was seated at a small wooden table with deep gouges carved into the top. Even during morning hours, there was little light in this dark little tavern. Joe ordered a beer, careful to keep his eye on Finley who sat there looking nervous, impatiently checking his Rolex every few seconds.

The bartender, a bald man with a scruffy beard and pudgy face, placed a frosted mug in front of Joe. "Thanks, bud," Joe said, handing the man a five-dollar bill and told him to keep the change.

Joe had taken only a mouthful of foam from the rim of the mug when the man Stephen Finley had come to meet appeared in a doorway beside the bar. He was a tall, thin man with olive skin and slick black hair. He wore an expensive silk suit that seemed entirely out of place in the rundown bar where he clearly was king. He checked his gold pocket watch, surveyed the room and then swaggered toward the table where Finley was seated. Approaching from behind, he laid a diamond-laden hand on Finley's shoulder, and Finley nearly jumped out of his seat with fright. Joe could tell that instilling fear in the feeble Stephen Finley amused the man.

The bartender placed a can of peanuts in front of Joe whose attention was focused on the table where Finley and the tall man sat. "That's the boss, Mr. Olivetti," the bartender muttered.

"Oh," Joe said shrugging his shoulders slightly in an effort to seem unconcerned. He chased a handful of peanuts with a drink of beer.

Taking a seat at the table across from Finley, Olivetti took a new deck of cards from his jacket pocket, removed the plastic wrapping and began dealing a hand of blackjack. Finley was explaining himself to Olivetti, who seemed oblivious to Finley's words and only continued to deal the cards. Olivetti looked up at Finley and said, "You want me ta hit ya?"

"What?" Finley asked, a look of sheer panic overtaking his face.

"The cards, Mr. Finley. Do you want another card?" Olivetti said.

Finley checked his hand. "Uh, no, I'll stay," he said embarrassed.

"Fine," Olivetti said. He pulled the face-down card from beneath a queen and flipped it over to reveal an ace. "Blackjack," he said. "The house wins. Now ya see, Finley, that's a lesson for a sniveling little bastard such as yourself."

"What's that, Mr. Olivetti?" Finley said, accepting Olivetti's insults without objection.

"The lesson is: the house wins. The house always wins, and *I am the house*."

"I understand, Mr. Olivetti. I really do," Finley said. "And I promise you, I will get you your money. I just need a little more time. The insurance settlement is coming through shortly."

"Two weeks," Olivetti said firmly. He gathered the cards from the table and got up to leave. He strode across the room. "Two weeks, Finley, and then..." he called out without turning around again. Olivetti paused before walking back through the doorway through which he had come. He dropped the deck of cards into the wastebasket beside the bar. "Then all bets are off." He walked through the door and was gone.

"Yes, sir, I understand," Finley called to him. "And thank you!" A look of relief washed over Finley's face, pale with fear. Having bought himself a little more time, Finley stood up and walked quickly to the door.

"Can I get you another brew?" the bartender asked Joe.

"I'm afraid one's my limit," Joe smiled. "Say, what was that all about?" Joe nodded his head toward the table where Finley and Olivetti had sat.

"Oh, nothing really. That guy comes in here all the time. Name's Finley, I think. Owes a tidy sum, from what I hear. Has a nasty little gambling habit. In hock up to his ears. But you didn't hear that from me."

Joe took the last drink from his beer and placed another five spot under his empty glass. The bartender retrieved the bill from beneath the glass and yelled, "Thank ya, bud!"

"Don't mention it," Joe said as he pushed open the door and walked out into the sunlight.

A nnie parked her truck along a narrow street in a blue-collar neighborhood on the edge of Knoxville, got out and walked down the sidewalk. She pulled a wrinkled slip of paper from the rear pocket of her jeans and read the address as she glanced at the numbers on the houses lining the street. "Well now, let's see where the famous Cass Belton lives," she mumbled. "Right there," she concluded when she matched the numbers on the paper to the ones on the porch post of a modest rancher with clay-colored vinyl siding. The entire house, except for the attached garage, was hemmed in by a four-foot chain link fence. Annie noticed Flo's old brown car parked a little farther up the street. Cass's car was conspicuously absent from the driveway, and she hoped she would find Barbara alone.

Annie took a deep breath and then unlatched the chain link gate and slipped into the yard. She had taken only a few steps toward the house when a large black German Shepherd came bounding around the side of the house. By the time Annie noticed the dog, it was already in mid-air. Before she could even turn to run, she felt a thud against her chest that took the breath out of her and knocked her to the ground. Instinctively, she tucked her head to her chest and rolled into a ball. She could hear the dog growling as its sharp teeth tore at her clothing. She cried for help for what seemed like an endless amount of time. Then, as quickly as it had begun, the attack ceased and Annie rolled over and looked up to find Barbara holding the straining, growling Shepherd by its collar.

Barbara quickly chained the dog to a porch post and returned to help Annie, who now lay sprawled on the front lawn looking up at the sky. Barbara knelt beside her and began checking her limbs for bites. Then she pulled a handkerchief from the pocket of her flannel shirt and wiped the blood from a long scratch on Annie's throat, which she knew had been made by one of the dog's claws. Barbara began unbuttoning Annie's oxford cloth shirt which immediately roused Annie from the foggy haze in which she had been floating. "What are you doing?" Annie cried, reaching up to pull the unbuttoned sides of her shirt together.

"Jus' tryin' to get a peek at yer tits," Barbara said. "I always wanted to get a look at 'em." A look of alarm passed over Annie's face, and then she realized Barbara was only kidding. They both began to laugh. "I'm looking for cuts, you crazy thing! Now hold still a minute." She rebuttoned the shirt and then helped Annie to her feet. "What in the world are you doin' here, Annie? That dog coulda killed ya, ya know." They passed the German Shepherd on their way into the house. "Annie, meet Maddie," Barbara said nodding toward the dog. "Maddie, this is Annie." The dog now lay on the grassy lawn looking placidly unconcerned and panting from the heat of the late afternoon sun. "Maddie was Cass's canine partner when she was a beat cop," Barbara explained.

"More like an attack dog, if you ask me," Annie muttered as she made her way up the steps to the front door.

"What are you doin' here anyhow?" Barbara asked opening the door and motioning for Annie to walk inside.

"I came to apologize to you," Annie admitted sheepishly, "you know, for the way I acted toward you last night."

"Aahh," Barbara said in a nasal tone, "that wasn't necessary, Annie. I was as much to blame for that little skirmish. I'm sorry, too. I really do appreciate all you're doing to help find out what happened to Julie. You're every bit the detective Cass is. It's just that, you know, Cass and I are gettin' to be good friends."

"Is that all?" Annie asked.

"All what?"

"Is that all you're getting to be? You and Cass? Just good friends?" Annie persisted, and then regretted having pried. "I'm sorry, I realize that's none of my business."

"Nope, I'm glad you asked," Barbara said returning from the kitchen with a first aid kit in one hand and a cold beer in the other. "Ya wanna beer?"

"No, thanks," Annie said appreciative of the care Barbara was showing her. "Ouch!" Annie winced as Barbara cleaned the wound on her neck and applied some antibiotic ointment and covered it with adhesive bandage.

"When did you have your last tetanus shot?" Barbara asked as she replaced the lid on the ointment and gathered the torn paper and plastic that had held the bandage.

"I'm current," Annie said.

"Good," Barbara said. "Now about Cass and me."

"It's really not necessary," Annie said. "I didn't mean to meddle in your affairs...uh, your business...oh, you know what I mean."

Barbara laughed and then swilled the rest of the beer. She plunked the empty can onto a coaster on the coffee table. "Cass and I are just good friends, Annie. You know, buddies. We like to hang out together but we're not romantically involved. She prefers a woman who's…oh, you know, foofy-poofy, whatever."

"Foofy-poofy?" Annie asked smiling.

"A lipstick lesbian, Annie. I mean, Cass's woman wouldn't have to be dressed in heels and a skirt all the time, but she certainly has to be more feminine than this butch, that's for sure." Barbara pointed her thumbs toward herself. "Now a woman like Lisa, she might even fit the bill for Cass. Hell, I like a more feminine woman myself."

"What about Julie?" Annie asked, skillfully ignoring Barbara's suggestion that Lisa might be a woman Cass would be attracted to.

"What about her?"

"Well, she wasn't, uh…isn't…exactly overly feminine."

"No," Barbara said, "but she's certainly a blame sight more feminine than I am, wouldn't you say?" Annie nodded, conceding Barbara's point. "Now I'd like to ask you a question."

"Okay," Annie said matter-of-factly, "shoot!"

"What do you have against Cass?"

The question took Annie by surprise and knocked the breath out of her nearly as much as Maddie had done only moments earlier. She pondered the question for a few moments and then offered Barbara as honest a response as she could. "It's not that I have something against Cass, Barbara. It's more about what I have against myself, my own personal hang-ups. I think it has something to with the recognition that never came my way, with the credit for accomplishments I believe I've been deprived of. For Pete's sake, Cass Belton gets credit for things she doesn't even do! Somehow recognition just falls in that woman's lap. No, it doesn't just fall on her, it chases her down!"

"Is that what this is all about?" Barbara asked in disbelief. "Annie, you're the most capable woman I know!"

"You really mean that?"

"Well, hell yeah, girl!   And if I know it, I can damn well guarantee you everybody else does, too!"   Barbara got up and slapped Annie hard on the back on her way to the kitchen to get another beer. "We ain't none of us gonna get all the credit we deserve for some of the stuff we do in life. And we can thank the good Lord for that, huh?" She returned with another beer and winked at Annie. "Annie, I'm sorry if I made too much of Cass. I didn't mean to hurt your feelings. I's just excited to have a new friend!"

"I'm sure glad we've cleared the air, Barbara!   Will you forgive me for being so nasty to you last night?"

"There's nothin' to forgive, Annie Oakley! We're friends, and if I have anything to say about it, we're gonna be friends for as long as I'm livin' and breathin'. Hell, no one's ever done as much for me as you and Lisa, and that's the truth!"   Barbara noticed the small tears forming in the corners of Annie's eyes.   "Now don't go gettin' all sentimental on me, woman! You get on home and I'll meet y'all back there later tonight."   Barbara saw Annie to the door and wrapped her arms tightly around her in a bear hug before pushing her out the door. Barbara called to the dog still chained to the porch post, "Say goodbye to Annie, Maddie!"   Compliant, the dog barked once.

"Goodbye, Maddie!" Annie said looking back over her shoulder as she made her way down the sidewalk. "See you tonight, Barbara! And thanks!"

Pixie was racing through piles of red, gold and orange leaves which Joe and Lisa were raking from under the maple tree in the front yard when Annie pulled into the driveway and rolled down her window. "Where've *you* been?" Lisa called to her as she picked up a handful of dried leaves and tossed them into the cab of Annie's truck.

"I went to Knoxville to visit Barbara," Annie said tossing leaves back out the driver's side window. "I needed to apologize for the way I behaved last night. She's coming back here later tonight."

"Good girl! I'm proud of you, Annie." Lisa said. "I'll fix something good for dinner."

Annie parked the truck in the drive and got out. Pixie left her piles of leaves to run and greet her. With the dog following close behind, Annie walked arm in arm with Lisa and Joe onto the front porch. Lisa and Annie sat on the porch swing while Joe eased into a bentwood rocker. "I followed Stephen Finley today," he announced.

Annie leaned forward with her forearms resting on her thighs as the swing rocked back and forth. "Anything interesting?"

"Yes, he's in hock to some sleaze ball mobster who runs a bar on the seedy side of Knoxville. Name's Olivetti. He gave Finley two more weeks to pay his debt. After that," Joe paused and moved his thumb across his neck in a slicing motion. "Finley's going to be pushing you hard, Annie, to get the insurance claim settled. He needs money and he needs it now."

"The way things are shaping up, Stephen Finley isn't going to get very much once the pension plan is re-funded and the company's debts have been paid. I don't know what he's expecting but I'll bet it's a lot more than what he actually gets."

"Then we'd better do something to get Finley out of here, because my gut tells me this Olivetti character isn't playing around. I really think he intends to kill Finley if Finley can't come up with the money he owes him." Joe pulled a corncob pipe from the pocket of his flannel shirt, filled it with tobacco from a new leather pouch and lit it.

"Where'd you get that?" Lisa asked.

"The pipe? Oh, I picked it up at a little tobacco shop in town."

Lisa closed her eyes and inhaled deeply. "Hmmm, it smells so good."

"Cherry tobacco," Joe added.

"Will you two pay attention? Let's get back to business," Annie ordered. "The clock is ticking for Stephen Finley, and the last thing we need is another corpse on our hands."

Joe puffed again on his pipe and winked at Lisa. "Okay, Annie," he said. "So what's next?"

"I honestly don't know," Annie said. She sat deep in thought for a few minutes. Then she got up from the porch swing and walked inside. Annie sat down on the sofa and, after hesitating for a long moment, she picked up the phone and dialed Cass Belton.

Early the next morning Barbara, Lisa and Joe were at the kitchen table slathering butter on blueberry muffins when Annie came in like a whirlwind, poured herself a cup of coffee in an insulated travel cup, and grabbed an apple from a bowl of fruit on the counter. "Where are you headed so early this mornin'?" Barbara asked. Before Annie could answer, a car horn began honking out in front of the house.

"That's Cass," she said, bending to kiss Lisa quickly. "Gotta go. I'm late. I'll tell you all about it this evening. By the way Cass is joining us for dinner tonight." Then she was out the door and they heard the car pulling away.

"Gee, she's in a good mood!" Barbara said. "And what's this about Cass? I can't believe those two are actually working together."

"Well," Joe said, "sometimes it takes Annie a while to get past herself. She gets in her own way sometimes, but once she gets back on track, she's fine."

"Now you've got to understand," Lisa added, looking at Barbara, "Annie and Cass are never going to get along one hundred percent of the time. They're two women with strong personalities and even stronger opinions. I'm sure they'll still fight like cats and dogs occasionally, but once Annie makes friends with someone, she sticks with 'em to the end."

"So who's making dinner tonight?" Barbara asked.

"I'll do it," Joe offered. "We'll give Lisa a break. Pass the muffins, please."

"Thanks, Joe," Lisa said, handing him the basket.

The phone rang, and Lisa got up to answer it. "No, I'm afraid Annie's not here," she said. "Who's calling please? I'll tell her you called. I'm not sure what time she'll be back. Yes, yes, I'll tell her it's urgent." She hung up the phone.

Joe got up and retrieved the coffee pot from the warmer. "Stephen Finley?"

"Exactly," Lisa said.

"Right on cue." Joe smiled. "More coffee anyone?"

C ass pulled away from the McDonald's drive-thru window with a large coffee in her right hand while her left hand alternated between the steering wheel and the button which controlled the electric window. Annie sat beside her in the passenger seat of the well-worn Crown Victoria, which had obviously seen better days. Antennae lined the top of the blue sedan like lightning rods across the roof of a barn, and although the car was otherwise unmarked, it was clear, to anyone who cared to look, that this was a police car.

Cass placed the coffee in her cup holder and, reaching into a white bag emblazoned with golden arches, she pulled out a bacon, egg and cheese biscuit, which she had promptly devoured by the time they reached the ramp to Interstate 40. She threw the sandwich wrapping back into the bag and wiped a greasy hand on her trousers.

"Here, use this," Annie said handing her a napkin. "You know that stuff will clog your arteries, don't you?"

"Ah, gimme a break, Annie. I usually have to eat on the run." Cass picked up the coffee cup again and took a drink.

"So where are we going?" Annie asked.

"After we talked yesterday, I went to the jail and had a chat with Sammy Dalton and his lawyer. Do you remember those self-storage units in Knoxville that were emptied before we could get to them?"

"Yes, that's always troubled me."

"Me, too. Sammy swears he had nothing to do with the disappearance of the lumber stored at Knoxville, and I don't know why, but I believe him."

194

"So what?" Annie said. "How does that help us?"

"I got to thinking about who else besides Sammy Dalton and Tom Finley knew that the lumber was stored there."

"Jim Wilkerson," Annie concluded.

"Exactly."

"I don't get it, Cass. Jim Wilkerson burned up in the factory fire."

"Well, the late Jim Wilkerson sold a piece of real estate to one Jim Waterson a couple days *after* the factory fire." Cass looked at Annie and smiled at her over the top of her coffee cup.

"So Jim's alive after all, is he?"

"I think so," Cass said. She signaled, changed lanes, and entered the exit ramp.

"But who is this Jim Waterson character?" Annie had the answer to her own question almost as soon as the words were out of her mouth. "Jim Waterson is Jim Wilkerson, isn't he?"

"Far as I can tell," Cass chuckled. "Waterson sounds an awful lot like Wilkerson. I think the old fart escaped the fire and decided he'd rather be someone else. You know, start all over with a fresh slate. That piece of property is pretty remote, way out in the mountains. I think Jim decided he was going to start a new life for himself."

Annie sank back in her seat, amazed at what Cass had learned and upset with herself that she herself had not thought to explore this angle. "So that's where we're going?"

"Yes, we're going to visit Jim Wilkerson a.k.a. Jim Waterson." Cass turned off the main road onto a secondary route that led upward into the Great Smokeys. After about half an hour, she slowed and left the paved secondary route, turning onto a poorly maintained dirt road that continued to wind upward.

"Are you sure you know where you're going?" Annie asked as they reached the top of the mountain and followed along its ridge. "This is more like a goat trail than a road," she mumbled.

"Anyone ever tell you you're a nag? Of course I know where I'm going," Cass replied. "And even if I didn't, it's not like there's any place out here to stop and ask directions."

"That's for sure," Annie agreed. "I don't believe I've seen one house on this road yet."

"You haven't," Cass said. "That's because this is an old fire tower road. Jim's place is probably the only house up here."

"How do you know he even has a house up here?"

Cass pulled a folded paper from the inside pocket of her jacket and handed it to Annie. "Jim Wilkerson applied for a building permit two weeks *before* the factory fire." Annie looked at the signature line on the bottom of the document where Jim's telltale 'X' was carefully printed.

Suddenly, Cass pulled to a wide spot at the side of the road. Then, putting the cruiser into reverse, she easily backed into a wooded clearing before cutting the engine. While Annie continued to stare intently at Jim Wilkerson's building permit, Cass removed the key from the ignition, tossed it into her jacket pocket and looked over at Annie. "You comin' or you just gonna sit here?"

"What?" Annie said startled from her thoughts. "Where are we going?" she asked, now realizing for the first time they were stopped in a secluded clearing.

"We're going to meet Jim Wilkerson," Cass said pushing the car door open with her boot.

"Why don't we just drive the rest of the way? I mean, the road's not great, but I think it's passable," Annie said. She leaned as she peered as far as she could down the dusty dirt road.

"You know, that's a great idea! Let me just get my bugle out of the trunk and we can play a little tune to announce our arrival!" Cass shook her head in disbelief as she leveraged herself against the steering wheel to push herself up and out of the cruiser.

"Okay, okay," Annie said, slamming her own car door shut and looking across the roof of the car at Cass, who had retrieved a revolver from under the seat. "You don't have to be so sarcastic. I get it already." Annie watched with interest as Cass pushed the gun's cylinder out and spun it to make sure it was loaded. She then shoved the gun into the shoulder holster beneath her jacket. "You're not planning on using that, are you?"

"I never *plan* to use it," Cass replied, "but it's nice to know it's there if I need it." She patted the area of her jacket which covered the holster, shut the car door and started walking down the road.

"Hey, wait up!" Annie called in a hushed tone. She retrieved her backpack from the passenger side floor and ran to catch up. Cass was already striding briskly down the dirt road to Jim Wilkerson's place, kicking up dust with practically every step. "I said, 'Wait up!' Didn't you hear me?" Annie said panting as she caught up to Cass.

"I heard you," Cass said smiling. Using her boot like a spatula, she slid her left foot across the dry ground and kicked a layer of fine dirt across the top of Annie's leather hiking shoes. Then, without breaking stride, she reached down, snapped the stem of a turtle weed and stuck the end of it in her mouth.

"Hey!" Annie objected. "Hey, that's not funny, Cass. Cut it out!" Mumbling under her breath, Annie walked to a patch of dry grass and leaves and stomped her feet to clean her shoes. "What the hell is wrong with you?"

Cass suddenly stopped. "Listen," she said.

"Don't change the subject!" Annie said, still wiping the sides of her shoes across the grass and leaves.

"Shhhhhh!" Cass ordered. "I said, 'Listen!'" Annie fell silent. Then she heard it. It was the sound of an engine. In a moment, she saw the front end of an old Ford truck winding along the dirt road toward them. Before Annie could say another word, Cass had grabbed her by the arms and thrown her into the woods. Stumbling, Annie turned her head in time to see Cass following right behind her.

Then, as she saw Cass crouch behind a tree, Annie felt her shin slam hard against something and she fell face forward onto the ground in a pile of leaves. Just then the two of them heard the truck pass by on the road. After a few moments, the sound of the truck's engine faded away, and Annie, still sprawled on the ground, felt a stinging pain in her leg. She lay there quiet for a few moments on the ground listening to the trees creaking like rocking chairs overhead and birds chirping in the cool autumn air. Cass collapsed at the base of the tree behind which she had been crouching, stretched her legs out in front of her and burst out laughing.

Annie raised herself up on her elbows and peered across the dead tree over which she had fallen, to see Cass casually breaking twigs and tossing pieces of them in Annie's direction. "You know, you're really beginning to irritate me, Cass. First you kick dirt on me, then you throw me into the woods and bust my leg, and all you can do is laugh at me!" Annie sat up, unlaced her shoe and rolled up the leg of her blue jeans to get a look at her injury.

"Aww, lighten up, Annie!" Still smiling, Cass stood up and dusted off the back of her jeans. She stepped over the fallen tree and sat down on it to assess the damage to Annie's leg. It was red and beginning to swell.

"I think it's only bruised," Annie said.

"Well, let's get you up and see if you can put any weight on it." Cass stood up again and took off her jacket and shoulder holster. Then she walked over to Annie who looked slightly fearful at her approach. Cass bent down and taking Annie's hand in her own, she pulled Annie's arm around her own neck, and with her other arm around Annie's waist, she pushed herself up from a crouched position, bringing Annie up with her. "Now let's see if you can stand on it," Cass said, but Annie was already bearing weight on the injured leg to see if it would hold her. She winced with pain. "That's it," Cass concluded, "I'm gonna go get the car and take you to the hospital. I just hope it's not broken."

"Just give me a minute, will ya?" Annie protested. "I know I can do this." She put the injured leg to the test once more, clenching her teeth to cope with the pain. Cass stood in silence as Annie hobbled two steps to the fallen tree she had tripped over and sat down to concede defeat. "All right, all right, go get the car."

"Annie, I'm sorry about this," Cass said. "It's my fault for being so rough with you."

"Ahhh, it's not your fault. I'm sorry this has screwed up our visit with Jim Wilkerson."

Cass left her jacket and holster on the fallen tree beside Annie and started toward the road. "Put on my jacket if you get cold before I get back," she ordered, just before she stepped out of the shaded woods and into the warm sunlight that covered the dusty dirt road.

Annie moved again to the ground, leaned her back against the fallen tree and turned her attention again to the sound of the trees creaking overhead. A squirrel with a nut in its mouth scrambled frantically from tree to tree in front of her. In the shade of the forest canopy that still had not lost all its leaves, Annie soon felt a chill, so she grabbed the jacket Cass had left and put it on. She glanced at her watch: 10:30. She lay her head back against the fallen tree to wait for Cass and fell asleep.

It was 2:00 p.m. when Annie awoke, her leg now throbbing with pain. "Cass should have been back here three hours ago," she mumbled, alarmed at what might have befallen her friend. She looked around until she saw a dead branch that curved sharply at one end. This she might be able to use as a crutch. Picking it up, she snapped off the smaller branches so that it was long and smooth, she tucked the curved end under her arm and limped a few steps to test the strength of her new creation. Satisfied her homespun crutch would help her get back to the car, she hobbled to the dead tree, picked up Cass's shoulder holster with the revolver tucked snugly inside and made her way toward the road.

By the time she reached the clearing where Cass had parked the car, Annie was exhausted. The gun in the holster may as well have been an anvil. She found the driver's door unlocked, but there was no sign of Cass anywhere. She sat down in the driver's seat to rest before deciding what she should do next. There were no homes for miles, so trying to walk back to the main road was out of the question. Besides, she wasn't sure she could make it that far on her bum leg. She wondered if it was broken.

Annie put on the shoulder holster and let her hand rest on the butt of the gun. It was smooth and cold. Momentarily imagining herself an Old West gunslinger, she drew it quickly from the holster, careful to keep the barrel pointed away from her. Joe had shown her how to shoot a gun when she was young, and although she remembered the experience, she couldn't recall any of his instruction. She shoved it back into the holster which she tightened to fit her. Then she stood up and did the only thing she knew to do. She started limping down the road toward Jim Wilkerson's.

The sun was setting when she reached the clearing at the end of the road. An old Ford truck was parked in well-worn ruts in the grass beside the log house, clearly still under construction. Smoke was rising from a new stone chimney and lights burned in the front rooms. Annie figured that Jim must have returned while she lay asleep in the woods, waiting for Cass to return. Not wishing to repeat yesterday's unfortunate encounter with Maddie, Annie hoped Jim Wilkerson had no dogs.

She hobbled quietly to the side of the house and peered in one of the windows. A man she could only assume was Jim Wilkerson sat comfortably in an overstuffed chair watching television. On the coffee table which he was using as a footstool lay a pistol, and a shotgun stood guard in the corner near the TV. In the rear corner of the room sat Cass Belton, bound and gagged, her head resting on her chin. Annie couldn't tell whether Cass was asleep, unconscious or dead. She sat motionless, crumpled in a heap against the wall, her hands tied behind her. Her knees were propped in front of her, and ropes bound her feet and legs together. Blood from the large gash in her forehead had stained the plywood living room floor still covered with sawdust. Annie looked but couldn't tell if Cass's chest was moving. If she was breathing at all, it was shallow.

Jim Wilkerson sat unphased, flipping through pages of the TV guide with one hand and impatiently pressing the buttons of his remote control with the other. Annie moved away from the window and took a deep breath. She leaned her back against the side of the house to shift her weight off the injured leg while she tried to decide what to do next. She knew that if Cass was still alive, she couldn't risk leaving her to get help. And if she was dead, she didn't want to risk letting Jim Wilkerson dispose of her body where they would never find it.

Annie placed her hand on the revolver in the holster and she knew what she had to do, but before she could move, she heard a car. Through the trees near the edge of the dirt road, she could see headlights, so she stumbled quickly toward the rear of the house to avoid being seen. Soon a black Mercedes coupe appeared and carefully made its way along the worn path that was Jim Wilkerson's driveway toward the house. Annie heard the car door slam. She waited a few more moments before peaking around the side of the house just in time to see Stephen Finley step onto the front porch. She heard him knock at the front door and thought this might be the best opportunity to catch Jim Wilkerson off guard.

She tried the rear door and finding it open, she abandoned her crutch and hobbled as carefully as she could into the kitchen. She could hear the two men talking at the front door. In frantic tones, Stephen Finley was telling Jim of his plight.

"I need that money now, Jim!" he cried. "Olivetti's gonna kill me if I don't come up with it soon!"

"What am I supposed to do, Steve? I'm waiting for the money from the buyer. He hasn't been able to come up with it yet, but he says he'll have it for us soon."

"I don't have time for that! Sell the lumber to someone else!" Finley's voice rose in pitch with every sentence.

"I can't do that," Jim said flatly.

"Why not?" Stephen cried.

"Stop actin' like some damned hysterical female!" Jim ordered, his face now flushed. "You'll get your money! Besides, I told ya on the phone I got bigger problems than that right at the moment."

"I don't know what could be more urgent than my life, Mr. Wilkerson. Remember? It's *my life* that's on the line here."

"Well it was my life on the line in that damned factory fire!" Jim roared. "And I put it on the line for you, Finley! How'd you like it if your wife of forty years stabbed ya in the back like Flo did to me? Layin' around with that damned Sammy Dalton for God knows how long, and then double-crossing me like she done! Locked me in that office in the middle of that awful fire. I still can't believe that good-for-nothin' bitch tried to burn me alive! But I showed her, yes I did! And it does my heart good to think ol' Sammy might go to prison for it all!"

Stephen Finley tried hard not to be overtaken with the fear he felt for the man who stood before him now, almost frothing at the mouth like a rabid dog. Hoping to quell the anger he saw in Jim Wilkerson's face, he infused his voice with as much calm as he could muster and chose his next words carefully. "Jim, I do appreciate all that you and Flo did for me. You moved all that lumber out of the factory. Then moved it again when that woman detective from Knoxville began nosing around."

"Well, that's why I called ya up here tonight, Steve. That detective came snoopin' around here this afternoon. Not sure how she knew I was up here. I guess I just got scared, that's all." Jim led Stephen Finley into the living room and pointed to the corner. "I tied her up. She sure put up a fight. Fights like a man, I'll give her that. Looks kinda like one, too. I think she's a queer."

Stephen Finley almost gasped at the sight of Cass Belton. He felt a queasiness in his stomach and his legs almost buckled under him. For a moment, he thought he might pass out from his fear. "Is she… dead?" he asked, afraid of what the answer would be.

"Naah, she's been coming in and out all afternoon, but I guess we're gonna have to kill her, don't ya think? I mean, it's hard to tell just what all she knows. We can't risk lettin' her go, Steve."

"We can't afford to kill a police officer, Jim," Finley objected.

"Far as I can tell, we can't afford not to," Jim replied.

"Well, you do what you want with her, but I don't want to know anything about any of it," Stephen said as he started for the door. "If you want to kill her, it's up to you. But I'm washing my hands of it, Jim."

Jim Wilkerson fought off the urge to lay his fist squarely across Stephen Finley's jaw. He followed Finley out the front door to the car, slamming the door behind him. Annie knew it was time to make her move, so she limped as fast as she could from the kitchen to the front corner of the living room where Jim's shotgun stood. She picked up the shotgun, moved to the front door and waited quietly for Jim Wilkerson to return. Cass was still slumped in the corner, but raised her head when Jim slammed the door and came inside, mumbling to himself. When he appeared in Annie's line of vision, she slammed the butt of the gun down hard against the back of his head, and Jim collapsed to the floor.

Cass watched with bleary eyes as Annie removed the ropes from Cass's feet and legs and used them to tie up Jim.

"The keys are in his shirt pocket," Cass said, her speech slow and slurred.

"The car keys?" Annie asked as she finished tying the last knot.

"No," Cass said, shaking her head, "my handcuff keys."

Annie couldn't resist teasing Cass just a bit as she retrieved the keys from Jim's flannel shirt pocket to free her friend's hands. "What kind of homicide detective lets an old man cuff her with her own handcuffs?" Cass chuckled then winced as Annie checked the wound on her forehead. "That's a nasty gash you got there, Ms. Belton, but as far as I can tell, your skull isn't fractured."

"That's good, I guess," Cass said

"Sure is," Annie said. "The last thing you need is *another* hole in your head."

"Very funny, Annie. Very funny."

Annie went to the back door and retrieved her homemade crutch from the place where she had parked it. She returned to the living room with a bag of frozen peas she had retrieved from Jim's freezer. She noticed that Jim Wilkerson was finally coming around.

He lifted his head from the floor and then lay it down again, his eyes still open. "I guess you girls really think you're somethin', don't ya?"

Annie did not give him the satisfaction of a response. She gingerly placed the bag of frozen peas against Cass's head to reduce the swelling. "I think we should call an ambulance for you," she said pulling pieces of dried blood from her friend's red hair.

"No way!" Cass objected. "I don't want the guys on the force to think I'm soft, Annie."

"You have a gash on the side of your head about four inches long. I don't think your coworkers will have any trouble believing you need an ambulance. "But," Annie paused, "if you want to act tough to impress your friends, I'll call one for myself. After all, my leg isn't in the best condition right now."

Annie turned to Jim, "So you're the one who stole the lumber and set the factory fire."

"What's it to you?"

"It's really nothing to *me*," Annie said, "but I suppose it meant something to Tom Finley. Didn't you feel the least bit guilty about burning down the business that had provided you with a job all these years."

Jim Wilkerson exhaled a laugh mingled heavy with disgust. "Tom Finley didn't give me nothing, nothin' but heartache, that is. What I got from him, I earned. Yes, that's right! I *earned* every last red cent of what I made slavin' at that factory all them years. Besides, the way I hear it, Tom was plannin' to burn the damn thing down hisself. I guess Steve jus' beat him to it!"

Annie thought about what Sammy Dalton had told her concerning Tom Finley's intentions of burning down his own factory.

"Mind you, Stevey ain't too bright. Matter of fact, sometimes he's dumb as a box o' rocks, but he was smart enough to know when to let go of a failure, and that furniture factory was a losin' proposition from the get-go."

"And I suppose you took the lumber from the Knoxville storage units, too," she continued.

"How d'ya think I built this house?" Jim said. "And Stevie's fool enough to think he's gonna get the money from it. I got news for him, though, 'cause it's all long been spent." Annie shook her head but didn't answer him. "Oh, don't gimme that self-righteous look, lady! Not until you've worked from dawn to dark every day of your life, scrapin' and savin', and you still never get ahead!"

Annie remained quiet, but Jim kept up his cathartic rant, as he tried in vain to wrestle out of the cuffs and ropes. "You know, you filthy women are all alike! Jezebels, all o'ya! I took care o' that woman o' mine for forty years, and what thanks do I get? She tries to burn me alive so she can run off with some sleaze ball insurance agent! One day she's cleanin' his office, and the next she's cleanin' his cock! Yes sir, she got exactly what was comin' to her, I tell ya!"

"Who do you think killed her, Jim?" Annie asked, hoping the bluntness of her question might elicit an unedited response.

For the first time since he had begun venting his grievances, Jim Wilkerson fell silent. The fierce resistance and frustration he had exhibited only moments earlier left his body and he fell limp, staring quietly at the ceiling. Cass glanced over at Annie as they waited in silence for more than a minute for his answer. "Dunno," he said finally. "Prob'ly killed herself. Who knows? Maybe Sammy Dalton did it. Doesn't matter now." He sighed and then closed his eyes, as if the effort it had taken for him to answer her question had entirely exhausted him. Annie now knew from Jim Wilkerson's manner, if not from his words, the identity of Flo Wilkerson's killer.

Then she took a seat on the sofa to rest her leg. She picked up the receiver from the phone on the end table, but before she could call for an ambulance and police, she heard what sounded like a drag race out in front of the house. She glanced out the front window, and through a thick cloud of dust kicked up by the cars, she saw two thugs pull a frightened Stephen Finley from a Lincoln Town Car and toss him easily onto the hood of the car. She heard Stephen pleading for his life, reminding the two henchmen that Olivetti had given him two more weeks to pay his debt. Annie's intuition told her that bad was about to turn to worse, so she quickly moved to get Cass onto her feet and out the rear door of the house only moments before these two well-dressed gangsters kicked the front door open. The larger man held Stephen Finley by the scruff of the neck like some heartless fiend dangling a puppy over the rail of a bridge before dropping it into the water below. Suddenly he let go, and Finley fell onto the floor next to Jim Wilkerson.

If the gangsters thought it strange that Jim Wilkerson lay cuffed and shackled in the middle of a seemingly empty house, they didn't take too much time to think about it. Instead, the taller of the two men pulled off his leather gloves and looked down on the two men with disgust. "Finish it," he said to his partner. He turned to leave the most gruesome part of their work to his subordinate, who pulled out a pistol from a holster under his jacket and placed the barrel first against the forehead of Stephen Finley and then of Jim Wilkerson. Two shots rang out and both Annie and Cass, now huddling together just outside the rear door, shuddered at the fate they knew had befallen the two men, but they were also somehow relieved that Jim had not had the opportunity to reveal they were in the house. After a minute, they heard a trunk slam, and then one of the thugs tramping around inside the house. Soon gasoline fumes reached the women's nostrils, and they realized what the henchmen were preparing to do. They heard a loud whoosh sound, then an explosion which blew the windows out of the cabin and engulfed the house in flames. Hundreds of tiny shards of tempered glass rained down on the two women like a shower of violent diamonds as they instinctively struggled together to get into the woods behind the house. Here they watched orange flames reach toward a pink twilight sky as the gangsters sped away.

It was almost midnight by the time Cass and Annie were able to get police to the still smoldering remains of Jim Wilkerson's house. While they waited, Annie sat with Cass at the edge of the woods and shone a flashlight on an empty red gasoline can that Olivetti's men had left overturned in the front yard. Cass sat beside her holding her own head in her hands. "How in the hell am I gonna explain to my captain why my handcuffs are locked around the wrists of a skeleton in the middle of a burned out cabin?"

"Maybe we could find and remove them before they get here," Annie suggested. Then again, we could try something really daring."

"What's that?" Cass asked, half-afraid of what Annie was going to propose.

"We could tell the truth. After all, we didn't do anything wrong here."

"Just doesn't look good, that's all. You know, having my cuffs on the wrists of a man shot and then burned while we sat in the woods doin' nothin'"

"What in the world could we have done, Cass?"

"I dunno," Cass said still holding her head in her hands like a heavy weight, her elbows propped on her knees. A light breeze blew the smell from the charred remains her way. Cass leaned away from Annie and began to gag. "Doesn't that smell make you sick?"

Annie knew that Cass was referring to what was to her the now familiar smell of burned human flesh. "Yes," she said.

Cass remembered that Annie was a funeral director by trade. "I don't know how anyone could get used to that. I guess you see some pretty horrible sights, huh?"

"No more than you, I imagine," Annie said staring at the heap of red hot coals that lay before her. "You never really get used to it. And if I ever do, then it'll be time for me to quit." Annie remembered how sickened she had felt when she discovered her boss Bill Williams, his wife Karla and their two small children slain in their own home. Despite the heat from the still-burning house in front of her, she felt a chill that brought goose bumps to her forearms and made the short cropped hair on the back of her neck stand up.

It was early the next morning by the time Annie and Cass had given their statements to police, had their scrapes and wounds treated at the local hospital, and returned home. Annie had called late the night before to let Lisa know she wouldn't be back before morning.

Pixie was at the kitchen door barking and wagging her tail when the Wilkerson's garage door rose and Annie and Cass pulled in. Excited, the dog ran to the kitchen door to greet them. Soon the kitchen door flew open and Annie yelled, "Hey, everybody! We're back!" Lisa, Joe and Barbara were in the living room watching CNN as Annie's crutches thumped across the kitchen floor and she appeared in the living room doorway.

"What on earth happened to you?" Lisa said, getting up to make room for Annie to sit down. "You didn't tell me you were injured."

Annie handed off her crutches and took her seat on the sofa beside Lisa. "I didn't want you to worry," she said, kissing Lisa lightly on the forehead. The kitchen door slammed shut and Lisa, Joe and Barbara looked at each other, puzzled by the sound until Cass, her head heavily bandaged in white gauze, stuck her head around the doorway into the living room.

"Dear heavens, this one looks worse than the first," Lisa cried. "We should have known better than to let these two go off on their own."

"What happened to y'all?" Barbara asked.

"You tell 'em," Annie said. She lifted her leg, now immobilized in a soft cast, and rested her foot on the coffee table.

Cass looked suddenly sheepish. "Well, it's a long story, really," she began.

"Do tell!" Joe urged. He retrieved his corn cob pipe from the pocket of his shirt, tapped the barrel against his palm, then put the end in his mouth. He didn't dare light it indoors because he knew that Annie would be unhappy with him.

Cass related all that had occurred at Jim's Wilkerson's cabin. "So the truth is, I got pistol-whipped and hog-tied. And if it weren't for Miss Annie here, I'm pretty sure I'd be dead right about now. You guys shoulda seen her. She was really somethin'!"

"It really wasn't any big deal," Annie said, half-embarrassed at Cass's accolades. Pixie stood dutifully beside the sofa, whining and nuzzling Annie's hand for attention now and again. "Okay, girl," Annie said to her finally, playfully tousling the hair on the Golden's head, "it's all right! Everything's going to be all right now." Annie tried to make herself believe that it would be.

B y mid-December, Annie had settled the insurance claim for Finley Furniture, and re-funded the pension and 401k plans of the employees. She had even arranged for the burial of Stephen Finley.

"So, when are we flying back to Santa Rosa?" Lisa asked. She carefully placed the urn containing the ashes of Jim and June Wilkerson into a white packing box and had just finished addressing it when Barbara appeared in the door of the kitchen.

Startled, Lisa stuttered, "I thought you and Joe were going into town."

"Already did," Barbara said as she lifted her leg over the back of one of the straight back chairs and landed hard on the seat. "Got back early. What's that you're mailing?"

"Oh, it's nothin', just a few pieces of pottery from Alewine in Gatlinburg. My mom likes handmade pottery, so I thought I might send her some for Christmas."

Annie took a sip from her coffee cup and waited to see if Lisa could sell this lie. Before Lisa could casually get the box out of sight, Barbara leaned forward and read the name and address written in large black letters on the top of the box: Julie Wilkerson, c/o Yvonne Roberts, 9435 Regency Row, Provincetown, MA.

"Oh," Barbara nodded. Lisa knew by the look on Barbara's face that the jig was up.

"Barbara, let me explain," Lisa pleaded.

"Lisa, you always were a bad liar," Barbara smiled. "It's okay."

"But," Lisa tried to interrupt.

Barbara placed her hand on Lisa's arm. "No, really, Lisa, it's okay. I understand. I know you and Annie were just trying to protect me, keep me from bein' hurt. And I love you two for that, I really do. You know, I sorta wondered whether Julie might've just run off. She hadn't been herself for a while. She was really quiet, you know, more than usual. I'd ask her what was wrong, and she'd clam up even more. I wondered if she might be gettin' tired o'me. I didn't really fit in with her educated friends. Hell, I know I can wear on peoples' nerves.

"Barbara, that's not so," Lisa offered.

"Like I said, Lisa," she continued, "you're a bad liar." The room was quiet for a few minutes. Annie noticed tears flowing from the corners of Barbara's eyes. She wiped them away with her shirt sleeve. "Gimme the box."

Lisa looked surprised at first, then pushed the white box across the table to Barbara.

Barbara got up from the table and went to the garage, returning with a shovel. She picked up the box with her free hand and Lisa and Annie followed her to the front door and out onto the porch. Barbara walked slowly down the steps and placed the box at the foot of the large maple tree in the front yard. "If it was me, I'd want to be laid to rest at home. What d'y'all think?" Lisa and Annie nodded, and joined her in the front yard. Barbara stepped on the top of the shovel and began to dig, while Annie and Lisa untaped the packing box and removed the urn. Barbara had only broken a sweat by the time the hole was deep enough. Casting the shovel aside, she dropped to her knees, motioning for Lisa and Annie to join her. "Annie, you wanna say a few words or a prayer or something?" Barbara reverently placed the urn in the earth as Annie flipped through her memory files for the right prayer.

Annie took a handful of earth and tossed it in on top of the urn. "Man, remember that you are dust and to dust you shall return. May the perpetual light shine upon them, and may their souls, and all the souls of the faithful departed, to the mercy of God, rest in peace. Amen." She made the sign of the cross.

"Amen," Lisa and Barbara said in unison as they clumsily crossed themselves.

The three women then pushed the soil back into the hole and patted it until it was firm. Barbara stood up, dusted the soil from the knees of her jeans, and picked up the now-empty packing box. "I'll write to Julie to tell her about her folks." she said. "So who is this Yvonne Roberts?" She pointed to the lettering on the packing box. "That name sounds kinda familiar."

The question took Lisa by surprise. Paralyzed by this unexpected question, she paused to consider how to answer. She looked to Barbara almost like a deer caught in headlights.

Before Lisa could answer, Annie stepped between the two women and put an arm around each. "Who wants to go to Dollywood's Smokey Mountain Christmas tonight?"

"I do! I do!" Lisa cried and took off running up the stairs and into the house.

"Good save, Annie," Barbara said smiling.

Annie winked at Barbara. "C'mon, let's go. Lisa's so excited, she might leave without us."

"Three and a half million," Barbara read from the brochure as she passed through the gate at Dollywood.

"Three and a half million what?" Annie asked.

"Lights," Lisa said without missing a beat. "That's how many lights are used in the displays during Smokey Mountain Christmas."

She walked ahead of the others, gazing at the white lights that illuminated tree branches throughout the park as bluegrass sounds of familiar Christmas carols filled her ears. Annie watched with delight as this woman she loved wandered child-like through this place that seemed to her filled with magic.

"Lisa, I'd like to see the little cabin you mentioned, you know, the replica of...."

"...the one Dolly grew up in! Sure!" Lisa grabbed her by the arm and led her to the wooden cabin in the center of the park.

"That's odd," Lisa said.

"What's that?" Annie asked.

"All of these people around and no one's going into it." "They're here to see the lights, Lisa. Most are probably just not interested in knowing Dolly's life history." Lisa glanced at Annie as if she had just committed blasphemy. "But I am!" she quickly added.

Lisa walked arm in arm with Annie up the stairs to the porch of the little cabin, with Barbara following behind.

Lisa seemed to Annie almost reverent as they stepped inside. As she had on previous visits, Lisa tried to absorb the details of the little cabin, imagining what her idol's life must have been like in such a space. Suddenly she found herself standing alone, so she turned to see where Annie and Barbara had gone and couldn't believe her eyes. She looked closely at the beautiful woman who stood before her in a velvet Santa suit and hat. She wondered if she were dreaming. The woman stepped toward her and put out her hand, "Lisa Cannon?" Lisa nodded. "Hi! I'm Dolly."

Lisa reached to take the woman's slender hand in her own. She could no longer fight the feeling of lightheadedness that had overwhelmed her at the sight of this woman she had adored from her childhood. Annie and Barbara heard a thud and came hurrying back inside from the porch to find Lisa lying unconscious on the floor.

L isa opened her eyes slowly, squinting at the light from the lamp on the end table at the other end of the sofa. Her eyes moved to the right. Her blurry vision now coming into focus, she recognized the woman sitting in the overstuffed chair beside the sofa. Barbara sat there flipping through the pages of a magazine, her legs crossed like a man, and jiggling her foot against her knee. "Hey, Annie," she yelled over her shoulder without taking her eyes off a shapely blonde she found particularly attractive in the swimsuit issue of Sports Illustrated, "Better get in here! I think she's finally waking up!"

Annie appeared in the doorway to the living room wiping her hands on a tea towel she had been using to dry the breakfast dishes. Lisa lifted her head, but it was so heavy that she quickly let it fall back against the pillow. Annie sat down on the sofa beside her and brushed the hair from Lisa's face. "Don't try to get up. Just lie there and relax."

Lisa closed her eyes again and then opened them wide. "What happened? Where's Dolly?"

"You took a fall," Annie said. "You were released from the ER late last night, and we brought you back here to the house. You've been asleep since then."

Lisa remembered the lightheaded feeling she had felt in the cabin. "I can't believe I passed out in front of Dolly. I'll bet she thinks I'm some kind of nut case."

Barbara and Annie exchanged concerned glances. "You took a hard hit to the back of your head, Lisa. I think you've been dreaming....you know, dreaming that you actually saw Dolly."

"It was not a dream, Annie! I'm telling you, I saw her! She even called me by name and shook my hand!" Now Lisa was sitting up and shouting. "She was dressed in a red velvet Santa suit and hat, and...," she paused, angry at the discomfort she saw on their faces. "Okay, okay, I can tell that you two don't believe me, but I know what I saw, and I saw Dolly Parton, flesh and blood, in that cabin with me!" Lisa's feet hit the floor with a thud. She stomped up the stairs and slammed the bedroom door behind her.

Lisa unscrewed the top of a bottle of ibuprofen she kept on her desk. She poured a few pills into her hand, popped them into her mouth, and chased them with a drink from a bottle of water. Then she picked up a stack of mail and began sorting it. She sliced open an envelope with a familiar return address. "Annie," she called, "there's a letter here from Barbara."

Annie walked down the hallway and looked in to Lisa's office. "Did you call about the MRI report?"

"Not yet," Lisa said without looking up. "Listen to this,"

> *Dear Annie and Lisa,*
>
> *The house seems empty without you all here, but I'm getting along all right. Last week I found a job here in Pigeon Forge that I like pretty well. I'm working as a desk clerk at one of the local hotels. The pay's not much, but it's enough to get by.*
>
> *Julie showed up at my door last week after I wrote to her about her folks. She kinda hinted she might like to get back together with me. Seems life ain't quite as rosy with that fancy professor friend of hers as she thought it would be. I told her I didn't think that'd be a good idea right now, but that maybe we could see each other for a while and see how things go. I guess it's just hard to trust a person once you've been burned.*
>
> *I thought you'd be interested to know that Sammy Dalton pleaded guilty to grand larceny and conspiracy. He'll be sent to prison for 10 years. The murder charge was dropped. Cass says that Flo Wilkerson's case will probably never be*

officially closed, but that since Stephen Finley's cufflink was found in the motel room, it's pretty well settled that he did it."

"Wait a minute," Annie interrupted. "I can't believe that after all we went through, Cass still thinks that Stephen Finley killed Flo Wilkerson. He couldn't kill a fly!"

Lisa rolled her eyes. "May I finish?"

"Sorry," Annie said. "Go ahead."

Lisa cleared her throat, turned the paper over and continued:

> *"Well, that's about all for now. Hope y'all can come to visit again soon. Take care and write or call when you can. Tell Joe and Pixie I said "Hi!"*

> *Your friend, Barbara*

> *P.S. to Lisa: Almost forgot, Julie asked me if you had gone to the Albuquerque Library. She said she left something for you there. I really didn't know what she was talking about but I said I would ask you."*

Lisa put down the letter and began searching frantically through her file drawers. "Annie, what did I do with that note?"

"What note?" Annie asked confused.

"The note! The note! You know, the one Julie left for me in the locker at Dollywood when she disappeared! I know it's in here somewhere." Finally, she opened an unlabeled file folder she knew she had used while she was in Tennessee. "Here it is!" She pulled the folded slip of paper from the middle of the file. She grabbed her car keys from the center desk drawer. "Wanna go with me?"

"Go where?" Annie asked.

"To the Albuquerque Library!" Lisa cried.

"I dunno," Annie said seeming disinterested. "Right now?"

"Yes, now, silly!" Lisa smiled.

"If it's all the same to you, I think I'll pass," Annie said.

"Suit yourself! I'll see you tonight," Lisa said closing the front door behind her.

Annie reopened the door and shouted, "Be careful!"

"I will," Lisa called. She waved as she backed down the driveway and then sped off.

isa scaled the sunny steps of the Albuquerque Library. Once inside, she surveyed the counter and remembered the first time she had visited this building. It was where she first had met and befriended Julie Wilkerson two years earlier. She pulled the scrap of paper from her pocket and looked at it closely again: **LLC-GO-2-AL-C-724.112.** What had for so long seemed a cryptic message impossible to decipher now became clear to her: ***Lisa L. Cannon, go to Albuquerque Library. See 724.112.*** Julie had wanted her to locate a specific book in the library. Lisa found the 700 series and when she located the volume bearing the numbers on Julie's note, she smiled as she pulled the book from the shelf. A familiar face stared up at Lisa from the dust jacket. It was the most recent biography of Dolly Parton. Inside the front cover was an envelope with her name on it. Returning the book to its place on the shelf, she carefully opened the envelope and removed its contents which consisted of a handwritten letter and another smaller envelope. She read the note first:

Dear Lisa:

By now, you know that I've decided to disappear. I didn't want to hurt Barbara, but I need to spend some time alone. An old friend of mine from college has agreed to take me in for a while, then who knows what's next for me? I just need some time—a lot of time—to sort out my life, and I can't do it while I'm with Barbara. It's something I have to do alone.

My reasons for my decision are many, and I don't expect you to understand but I hope you won't hold it against me. I have been making plans to do this for a while now.

I have been in counseling for more than a year now for a situation that occurred when I was a child. The details really aren't important, but when I was eight years old, I saw my father and another man named Sammy rape and kill a woman whose name I still do not know. He never knew that I saw what he had done. I've been tortured by this memory ever since, and until recently, I was terrified to tell anyone.

Last June, I decided to tell my mother about what I had seen. At first, she didn't believe me. But after a few weeks, she called me to apologize. She said she had remembered some things that made her believe I was telling the truth, and that she thought she knew the identity of the murdered woman. Turns out some local woman went missing around the same time I saw what I saw. Mom started putting things together and, finally, she decided to confront my father. Naturally, he has denied everything, but I think he's running scared. She says I shouldn't worry anymore, that she's making plans to take care of everything. Frankly, I don't know what she can do, but I can't worry about that now. I just need to get away.

Lisa, I'm sure we'll see each other again someday. Until then, I hope you enjoy the enclosed.

Love,
Julie

Stunned, Lisa sank to the floor, leaning against the stacks, Julie's letter still in hand. After a few minutes, she folded the letter, got up and walked to her car, still thinking about what Julie had written. She regretted the harshness with which she had judged her friend. Inserting the key into the ignition, she remembered the smaller envelope and retrieved it from the passenger seat where she had thrown the letter and the envelope with her name on it. She chuckled as she pulled two season passes to Dollywood from the envelope. She kissed them quickly. "Looks like we'll be going back to Tennessee again next year," she said to herself as she left the parking lot and headed back home to Santa Rosa.

www.ingramcontent.com/pod-product-compliance
Lightning Source LLC
Chambersburg PA
CBHW061355280526
45784CB00001B/270